Ciarán Hodgers (he/him/his) is an Irish spoken word poet based in the UK. His debut poetry collection Cosmocartography, published by Burning Eye Books in 2018, was shortlisted for the prestigious Rubery Book Award and toured the UK & Ireland, featuring in national media on both sides of the pond.

Winner of the Sean Dunne National Young Writer Award in 2010, an International Pangaea Poetry Slam Champion 2015 and the Word War 3 Slam Champion, he has been shortlisted for the Pushcart Prize, OutSpoken Prize for Poetry and longlisted for the Not The Foreword and Gingko Eco-poetry competition.

Published internationally in journals, anthologies, festivals, exhibitions and curriculum texts, he is also an experienced workshop leader and creative mentor, supporting people with their creative practice towards publication and a sustainable, consistent creativity.

CW01501633

ciaran.hodgers.071189
@gmail.com

Also by Ciarán Hodgers:
Cosmocartography (Burning Eye, 2018)

Solastalgia

Ciarán Hodgers

Burning Eye

For Johnny and Bernie,
whose garden was my first paradise

CONTENTS

Solastalgia

INTRODUCTION

Hello again, dear reader. What a joy it is to meet again in these pages.

The title of this book is a word that has stuck with me ever since I first came across it a few years ago. Coined by philosopher Glenn Albrecht, *solastalgia* describes the existential dread we face when our impact on the natural world comes starkly into focus. It might remind you of nostalgia, which is described as a pain for the past; well, the *solas* (from the Latin *sōlācium*) relates to comfort, so solastalgia might be better understood as a 'comfort pain', or a 'pain of home' – the pain of seeing the home of our planet negatively affected.

This collection roots its context in solastalgia as much as its content. When I was about six or seven years old, I was walking through my parents' sitting room one weekend afternoon, where my dad was indulging in a documentary about space and the planets in our solar system. I found myself in the crossfire of a sentence that would change me deeply. I paraphrase: '…and as the sun is constantly expanding, scientists estimate that it will eventually consume and destroy planet Earth in around five billion years.'

It was so final, so absolute, so unavoidable. Without the tools to process or understand this existential dread, creativity, as it so often does, sprang up where my heavy heart and this troubled world met. It gave me the opportunity to transmute it into something beautiful, something that could connect me with others to feel less alone, and perhaps something that could make things in the real world even just that little bit better.

I have been guided in developing this book by a lineage as old as the planet itself: the many writers who've spent their lives giving thought and nuance to the natural world and our relationship to it. It supported and deepened my connection to Irish and Celtic culture. The work hopes to connect to those who are situated within these lineages and offer a bit of gratitude for the wisdom and beauty they've carried for us.

The role of creativity in my life as a process of healing, of expressing oneself (in the many definitions of that phrase), was put to the test a few years ago when I was experiencing an intense and debilitating creative fallow. I decided to bring the topic of creativity to my counsellor for exploration and, if you are a creative person familiar with the counselling process, I would highly recommend you do the same. For me, there was something powerful about understanding my creativity on a deeper level: how it functions, when it breaks, and how it affects me in my day-to-day life. I felt the counselling process was an apt and perhaps unexplored structure for a collection of poems that look towards healing, the physical room of a session giving space to a new kind of language.

The voices, then, that do the speaking of the poems in this collection are sometimes my own, sometimes that of the planet, sometimes flora or fauna, sometimes an element or process that plays out in our world. They are asking how we, as a community of beings, can heal from what hurts us. While it's not a climate change book in the strictest sense, it does consider climate change as a traumatic event, as a mode of relationship, as a symptom of something much deeper, as a challenge to overcome. While it does touch on the practical side of things, the supply chains, emissions levels and economics, this book is more about the deeper spiritual, psychological and emotional work needed to heal, about nurturing relationships between ourselves and the more-than-human world. I think David Abram said it much better in his seminal work *Becoming Animal*:

> *Poetics, in this sense, would become the practice of alert, animal attention to the broader conversation that surrounds, to the utterances of sunlight and water and the thrumming reply of the bees, or the staccato response of a woodpecker to the hollow creaking of an old trunk and the attempt not to violate this wider conversation every time that we speak, but to allow it, to acknowledge it, and sometimes to join it.*

There is an inherent paradox to writing about this when, as we so often find, it is the transience and embodiment of speaking that connects us to landscape, through our own experiences and the wisdom offered by traditional oral cultures. I think this is why it's so lovely to be back with Burning Eye Books for this collection, as they sit wonderfully astride a similar paradox, of publishing performance poetry. When seeing a square peg and round hole, we ask ourselves how might it fit, rather than deciding, without imagining, that it won't.

I've had many great opportunities along the way that have helped shape and mould my mind into a space that could receive the wisdom of the world around me and best support me in speaking some of my own back out to it. Aside from the usual plethora of books, podcasts, magazines, movies, music and artwork that have fed my enquiry and exploration, I am thankful to those who've worked with me on residencies, performances, commissions, workshops, mentoring and other projects, giving me a gauntlet with which to sharpen my vision. I am especially grateful for the glorious chance to spend two weeks travelling with the inimitable Victoria McNulty as part of Edinburgh Book Festival's Outriders Project, run by Jess Orr; this was a completely unique and invaluable experience, and I will probably never know how deeply it affected me and my writing.

By the time you are reading this, this work will no longer belong to me. This cloistered little manuscript that has been growing slowly like moss on a boulder or lichen up a tree will soon be given over to you. I hope you can receive it with a happy and curious heart, that it can help you find reciprocity in the planet. Selfishly, I also hope that it will be neither too long nor too winding of a road until next time, and thank you.

Ciarán Hodgers
Dudley, June 2023

P.S. You can find a list of books that have, in one way or another, inspired this collection at bit.ly/ciaranhodgerssolastalgia

P.P.S. Support local booksellers.

EPILOGUE OF A BREAKDOWN

I hope this email finds you well. I'm writing to see if you have any appointments available. I think I should come and talk to you about what's been going on.

You see, I'm worried that I am becoming a butterfly pinning itself to a pristine white card. Fret that the carefully coloured shimmer on my wing will cause barely a neuron to fire when a different version of myself looks in.

I will become a bear cub suspended in formaldehyde. An immature maul, feral but stunted, all pity and rage plucked like thorns from a paw that won't have been held for months by then. Hibernating in the potential of a seed, waiting to be dexterous enough to shape it into something useful and then wallow in its tender, breaking promise.

I will become the whale skeleton hanging from the ceiling, all blubber melted for distant warmth, a starved scarecrow in an ancient sea. I'll watch over their sins as they pass, crucified on the knowledge that they'll no longer be accounted for and this hall will turn into an altar of forgotten blood.

I will become the partly reconstructed elk, retrofitted from a poor memory while they were on the train to come and see me. A slapdash Polyfilla puffing out the negative spaces of something once alive, cradling the tender structural integrity to hold long after it gave out; each falseness a ruby in my antlered crown.

I will become the taxidermied fox whose eyes look more glued on than set in place, the frizz in the whiskers, the paunch torn from too much sawdust. A mockery of a self, resurrected with clippings from someone else's manuscript, and I will want to blink so damn badly under the glare of these overhead lights.

I will become an aviary of mute nightingales, a silent case of dulled iridescence, fixed to branches only ever meant to be a temporary perch. Songs I'll forget the taste of will haunt those halls, pinging from pockets in a unison of hollow air I'll no longer be able to organise into staves.

I will become the object label explaining what it is they're looking at. Meaning by proxy, useful only to commute elsewhere. Flimsy context, gone as soon as they'll go; lonely epitaphs; a rusted key for a broken lock.

I will become the room of a colony's loot, every stolen gift, every body displaced from its grave. A collection only of wanton ravages that I will gaslight into glory, God and a geography written with a pen filled with someone else's blood, waiting for justice to come and scour me hollow.

I will become that emptied exhibition, not even a landlord of dead things, just the space they would inhabit if they were at all worth showing. I'll be under construction, out for maintenance, on loan to someone else.

I'll be mostly available Mondays and Tuesday but can do sessions after five the rest of the week. Are you still doing them online? Thanks for your time, yours sincerely.

We only want the earth.

James Connolly

DIRGELINGS

a found poem of species lost due to human activity

Arabian ostrich / Ascension crake / Atlas wild ass / Aurochs / Atlas bear / Big-eared hopping mouse / Bluebuck / Bramble Cay melomys / Broad-billed parrot / Bubal hartebeest / Bulldog rat / Bushwren / California grizzly bear / Canary Islands oystercatcher / Cape lion / Caribbean monk seal / Caroline parakeet / Carpathian wisent / Caucasian wisent / Cebu warty pig / Chadwick Beach cotton mouse / Chatham bellbird / Chatham fernbird / Colombian grebe / Colpocephalum californici / Cuban macaw / Delalande's coua / Dodo / Domed Mauritius giant tortoise / Domed Rodrigues giant tortoise / Dusky seaside sparrow / Eastern elk / Eiao monarch / Epioblasma haysiana / Erica warhami / Felicola isidoroi / Formosan clouded leopard / Goff's pocket gopher / Gravenche / Great auk / Guam flying fox / Gull Island vole / Haast's eagle / Heath hen / Hemigrapsus estellinensis / Huia / Japanese Otter / Japanese seal lion / Kangaroo Island emu / King Island emu / Laughing owl / Lesser moa / Lyall's wren / Macquarie parakeet / Madeiran scops owl / Malagasy crowned eagle / Martinique amazon / Mauritius blue pigeon / Mauritius scops owl / Merriam's elk / Moa / Mount Glorious day frog / Nesoryzomys darwini / Nesoryzomys indefessus / New Zealand greater short-tailed bat / New Zealand musk duck / New Zealand owlet-nightjar / New Zealand quail / Newton's parakeet / Norfolk kākā / Noronhomys / North Island giant moa / North Island snipe / O'ahu nukupu'u / O'ahu 'ō'ō / O'ahu 'akialoa / Oryzomys antillarum / Pantanodon madagascariensis / Paschalococos / Passenger pigeon / Piopio / Quagga / Ratas Island lizard / Réunion giant tortoise / Robust crow / Rocky Mountain locust / Round Island burrowing boa / St. Croix macaw / San Marcos gambusia / San Martin Island woodrat / São Miguel scops owl / Schomburgk's deer / Sea mink / Small Mauritian flying fox / South Island snipe / South Island stout-legged wren / Southern black rhinoceros / Steller's sea cow / Syncaris pasadenae / Syrian elephant / Syrian wild ass / Tarpan / Tasmania emu / Tecopa pupfish / Thicktail chub / Thismia americana / Javan tiger / Toolache wallaby / Tristramella intermedia / Upland moa / Wake Island rail / Western black rhinoceros / Western Lewin's rail / Xerces blue

stri   /   ke /   / u   s /
        /   /   /
        /   /   /   /
        /   f r   /   o   /
        /   m   /   /   th
        /   e /   r   /   e
co   /   rd/ h   / ol
      /   /   / D
  u /   /   s   to /
        /   y   o /   /
        /   /   /
/   u   r /   / Grave
/ G   /   o /   n   e / H   ea   /
        /   r   t   s /   /
        /   / K   e /   e /
/   /   /   /   p
/   o /   /   u
    /   r   /   /
    /   /   / N   a   /
        m   e s / Ne   a   r
/   and   /   let   /
  al   l /   t   /   /   h
/   ls   mo /   /   u
/   /   n   / r   / n
        i n /   /   g   g o /
/   a   /   s   a   d / Ré   a   /
    /   M   / R
/   /   /   /
        /   e   /   m   e /
m   /   /   /
              /   b   er   /
      /   /   /   /
/   /   u /   s /   /
        /   /   ache w   / i t
      /   /   /
hi   /   t   /

DEAD ICE

A letter to the future
Ok is the first Icelandic glacier to lose its status as a glacier.
In the next 200 years all our glaciers are expected to follow
the same path.
This monument is to acknowledge that we know
what is happening and what needs to be done.
Only you know if we did it.

Andri Snær Magnason, text on a plaque commemorating
Okjökull, the glacier on Ok mountain, Iceland

White-knuckled and patient,
even your dying was an exercise in endurance.
We printed your epitaph in copper
to offer it some of that longevity,
but also as a bluff,
urging future eyes to scowl
and spark us with incendiary guilt.

You were abdicated into lank,
the title shrank from officialdom
and that crown of glistening white
surrendered gossamer down the mountain,
acquitting bodies, bacteria,
methane and mercury from your preserving hold.

Whether the hollow that will emerge from your sinking
will amplify the drawn-out eulogy or not,
it will speak on our behalf regardless
and answer the question we buried you with,
an audience only in aftermath.

You were born from magma and momentum
but wizened into something slow and quiet,
unnoticed at first, unheeded as it went
until all these frozen thrones
insurrect themselves into seats of nowhere at all.

THE WHITE HART OF BOOTLE

Majestic amidst the terraced dust,
he lit up the red brick and mossy roof tiles.
My eyes fixed like a visitation
on the little myth pacing past my window.
He made this small world feel big again,
as if wonder could still exist,
as if it could still surprise me,
as if the calluses of a cynical heart
could just pop off.

Though they taped off where they felled him,
his blood, pooling in the concrete,
escaped the confines of their dirty work,
breaking that shrunken part of our hearts
where we allow ourselves to dream.

I don't believe them
when they say
there's nothing to see here,
move along, please,
as a desperate breath escapes
and the streets return
to their dulled and ordinary colour.

CLEARING

We are both ourselves and the trees.
Katie Holten, 'Deciphering Words in the Woods',
Emergence Magazine, 20 November 2020

If I think about it too much
I can forget what it feels like
    to be a clearance:
to have a body   that is disappearing
      bit by covert bit,
unable to point to any   specific trunk   or limb
and say
it was   here
it was meant   to be here
why is it   not here?

If I strain,   I can subtle   the thinning   of spirit
like a book   where all the letters fade
     and you read   by their serifs   instead;
meaning   cobbled   in detritus,
     terminal edges   not yet vanished
gathered   for scraps.

        If I want,   I can ignore   how
        I am   unlanguaged,
how the mind   comes to be
bone-cracked
       timber,
why dreams   loosen   like soil
and   become
diaspora   to the slept.

    I don't have to feel   this taproot,
        this hand,
           this child's hungry mouth

flexing for something   to root in,

                                    grasp for,
                                    latch onto

amidst that   deep,

                                         dark
                                         nothing

          of soil

that has

                                         become
                                         a

                                    self.

                                         but
m   ay   be
                                              l
      s   ho   ul   d
                                         s
            t
o   p   t
      o   fe

      e   l   b
                e   f
            o
re
            l

      d   i   s
                        a   p
      p

            e   a   r

c
o
m
p
l
e
t
e
l
y

GOLEM

Kneeling like a convert
to the body in the soil
(and the body of it),
fingernails trowel mulch
towards dirt damp as clouds,
where lovelines grime themselves
in the succour, swell and juice of buckling clods
squeezed from my closing fist,
fashioning a human from the humus.

Itchy for the grasp of another bulb,
under the stubble, lies the muscled mud beneath
that I knead into mycelial sinew
hoping it might pulse back,
but, exhumed,
only slips wet trenches down my palms
in rivers of sediment tracing outlines
that, once, were kissed clean.
I feel the small depression of a held hand
removing itself.

Our first skin was silt,
so why not make a man out of land now?
I roll this poem up into a scroll,
slip it into his mouth like a spell
to magic the mound into movement,
have it push back against my weight,
but the paper just blots and wrinkles.
He would need more than *hymn*, as it happens,
and the name of God melts into the mire.

I unpick fingernails for days,
inhaling the sweat of that deep, dark turf,
and look at the mucky men
lying like graves across the green,
a reminder of how words can't always hold you
the way you want them to.

EURIPUS

The barman's pour not enough,
this river's slick torrent, solid as marble,
should, I thought,
crack me when I land.

Just behind the bend
town makes way for bed.
The only brightness halogen:
streetlamps a string of fairy lights,
taxis pass like slow comets,
the halo of a cradled cigarette,
but skywards, the sliced silver scythe of a moon,
stars pulsing in a grievous chorus,
light heavy as sinking pebbles.

You can either move with the water's force
or against it.
Struggling is a refusal;
floating takes strength,
so does breathing,
swimming upstream
and, always,
leaving.

SURFACING

for Taryn

When she told me how you went
I heard a twig snap beneath my foot
like the sound of it was your name now
and I was summoning you
from a sea of trees.

I saw you not as softly spoken
as I had thought you to be,
just drowned out, muffled by a mind
too heavy to float,
so you climbed
to drop like an anchor instead.

By the time the bubbles surfaced,
the wreckage that had been praying to be found as treasure
became testimony instead.
To salvage is past tense,
happens after the fact, the crash, the sinking,
and by then the shimmer of drowning
showed you something different when you looked up:
the lips of waves beyond the branches,
an oar, a doorway,
the moon an exit sign above.

VITRIFY

Mount Vesuvius eruption 'turned victim's brain to glass'.
Nicola Davis, The Guardian, 22 January 2020

I hope sleep kept you,
mercifully tightened its grip
as your lungs boiled into soap,
as bones singed to parchment,
as the brain we hold in our hands now,
filled then with the sand of dreams,
became glass.

We turn your thoughts like a prism,
scrying through obsidian whorls of history:
a thick, sculpted oil
dotted with the stars of your slumber.
Are those you thought of
petrified into its concave
like photographs, afterglows
or Hiroshima shadows?

What frescos will survive
when I am ash, or have I been painting
the ceiling of my skull
with invisible ink all this time?

I need to imagine
something beautiful can endure
beyond the end of all things.
Perhaps even because of it.

UNPRECEDENTED TIMES

after Emily Berry

I pluck mould off the bread before popping it in the toaster,
exhume the mummified tea bag
where it's been drying on the windowsill.
Pop in an extra spoon of sugar to balance out the taste,
shake the carton so the milk won't curdle in my cup,
security tag rattling like a dull cowbell off the cold, patterned plastic,
and I turn the kettle off at the wall when it is done.
Switches have become the enemy these days;
before I leave any room
I find myself scanning for those little red squares,
like dabs of blood on white tissue.
They can only take so many nicks out of me
before I am drained dry.

I calculate the cost of commuting.
The laptop will need charging
and the house will be freezing
and the trains are all on strike.
Can't afford a car, so you can forget about the cost of fuel.
Each moment chops parts of my daily allowance of existence off
and hands it to them,
asking, will this do?
Will this keep the market afloat long enough
for the lifeboats to arrive?
But we've been drowning for so long now
we've started offering driftwood
to the stormy skies in benediction
instead of waiting for help to come.

Later I'll recline by the oven as dinner cooks
like a tourist on a lounger by the pool
and watch TV on a phone I charged in the office
to forget the sharp shelf of the day lying across my shoulders
and that twitch that's sprung up in my right eyelid again,
before protesting the dark bedroom ceiling

that speaks with the same insidious, manufactured concern
I hear in the prime minister's voice,
telling me I'm to blame,
if only I worked harder,
until I wake to a world striving to convince me
everything is as steady and sure as the seasons
and what's worst of all,
I'm starting to think they might be right.

YOU CAN'T MAKE PROFIT ON A DEAD PLANET

Pointing to a heatmap
that spills like a wound
carved up the country,
do they feel even a little smug?
Happy for the airtime
when the weather is all we have to talk about.
But it's not LA, Australia or Brazil.
Today it's Kent that's on fire.
It's London's runways that are melting,
and ITV presenters telling us
to put mashed sweet potato under our armpits
if we find we're starting to smell.

I remember Florida,
how the water would boil straight off your skin,
roads undulating like a Sahara,
but today it was a wren lingering in the bird bath,
two young boys in the backseat of a car
dressed in stuffy, black blazers
behind a hearse.

Others settle into deckchairs with coolers full of beer
or lathe Factor 50 on behind blackout curtains.
Facebook warns me not to walk the dog I don't have
between ten and six
and I am held at gunpoint by how the urgency of doom
is met with the quiet practicality of making do.

Life goes on as normal:
celebrities continue to take seventeen-minute flights,
my pension still funds extraction,
the carbon reduction training goes on blaming me personally,
government persists in cosplaying as *Black Mirror* villains
and twenty-five companies keep doing the worst of it
as if they've found a way to make profit on a dead planet.

This is what it feels like to live
in the foreword of a dystopia,
stuck between twenty-four-hour news cycles
that give us so little actual storyline
that we're not really invested
in what happens at the end.

HANDWASHING

I am standing in the middle of the office bathroom;
the fluorescent lights burn away any shade
into clean, corporate concision.
I am paralysed in its glare,
hands dripping soapy water onto the floor
an underpaid cleaner will have to sort later today.

Paper towel or machine?
Paper towel or machine?
My instinct says machine,
because a paper towel was part of a tree once,
but then again I don't know who supplies this building's energy
and could using the machine be worse?
What if the paper towels are made from recycled materials?

A bead of sweat crawls down my temple
as my hands melt onto the lino floor.
I resign myself to flapping my hands dry,
listening intently for approaching footsteps,
wondering if I'm actually as crazy as I look.

TWO WEEKS IN THE SUN

*Tropical forests in the Americas are undergoing rapid
conversion to commercial agriculture, and many migratory
bird species that use these forests have experienced
corresponding populations declines.*
Bennett, Leuenberger, Bosarreyes Leja, Sagone Cáceres,
Johnson and Larkin, 'Conservation of Neotropical migratory
birds in tropical hardwood and oil palm plantations',
PLOS One 13(12), 2018

Two weeks in the sun feels too brief
for it to only come once a year,
but you were all-inclusive this time.
Found yourself awake first thing to beat the morning pool rush,
towel ready to throw over the first available lounger,
though it took a few days to find the best spot:
> maximum sun exposure,
> proximity to the bar,
> paddle pool in eyeline.

The smell of coconuts follows you home;
the orange plane is much less festive on the return.
You'd almost forgotten where you'd parked
or even how to drive, you'd switched off so completely.

Slowly, the novelty of the fortnight washes off like unstubborn sand
as you drive through the same familiar streets,
life waiting like an inevitability at the end of your road,
but when you turn the corner of your estate,
something feels not quite right.
It's only when you pull up to your driveway
that you find your house is gone.
Not like it's been destroyed by flood or fire,
no wreckage to describe what happened,
just simply gone
like it was never there in the first place.

WHITE GLADIS

Orcas have attacked and sunk a third boat off the Iberian coast of Europe, and experts now believe the behavior is being copied by the rest of the population.
Sascha Pare, 'Orcas have sunk 3 boats in Europe and appear to be teaching others to do the same. But why?', *Live Science*, 18 May 2023

Isn't it funny how
we named the behaviour of a wild, frightened thing
revenge?

She's never met Free Willy,
and I doubt she's doing it for Shamu.
She's hardly screaming 'Eat the Rich'
when she charges toward them.

I think it's probably a lot less complicated than that,
because I recognise the fervent rage of each crashing,
the need to chew yourself out of each trigger.

She remembers those other names we gave her:
wolf of the sea, fish tiger, *skana*, *polossatik* –
killer demon, feared one –
and she's reminding us
that the world will bite back,
should we ever give it cause.

WACKAGING AS METAPHOR FOR INTRUSIVE THINKING[1]

Hi. I'm a banana. You know me, right? ~~Workers earn less than 10% of the banana's total value~~. And I know you'd be rather be having a sausage roll or slice of cake for lunch today, right?. But you're here, you've picked me up, good for you! ~~Work is usually casual, temporary or on a daily basis with reduced trade union protections as a result~~. Anyways, you're probably not bothered about reading this product description if you're actually buying a banana for breakfast. ~~Workers can put in over eighty hours a week and often earn less than a living wage~~. You're all about utility, right? You're on a mission here, and I'm here to help. Wait till you get a load of my nutrition value: I pack a lot of vitamin bang for your buck. ~~Monocultural production damages ecosystems~~. Potassium, vitamins B6 & C, and in a slim 89 calories that'll save a lot of syns for a cheeky glass of vino later. ~~More money is often spent on agrochemicals than on labour~~. Technically, I'm a berry, not a fruit, so you can drop that in your next pub quiz or awkward family dinner. Oh, and we share about 50% of our DNA, me and you. Weird, right? ~~Large quantities of chemicals end up on workers' skin, in their homes and on their food~~. Like there's some banana ancestor that goes way back to a time before we split up, evolutionarily speaking. Be sure to dispose of my peel responsibly, and not on the ground waiting for someone to trip over it like a cartoon character. ~~Exposure to agrochemicals can result in depression, breathing problems, cancer, miscarriages, sterility and birth defects~~. Enjoy!

---

1 Struck-through information sourced from Banana Link: bananalink.org.uk

MONTHLY CARBON AND ACTIVITY REPORT

For all calculations, please round up to the nearest unit specified and input dates from the previous calendar month.

How many times did you travel for work?
What mode(s) of transport did you use?
In total, how many miles did you travel for work?
How many times did you travel for leisure?
What mode(s) of transport did you use?
In total, how many miles did you travel for leisure?

How many plant-based meals did you consume?
How many were cooked at home?
How many were eaten out?
How many grams of meat did you consume?
Of this, how many grams was red meat?
How many grams of animal product (milk, cheese, honey, egg etc.) did you consume?

How many kilowatt hours were used to power your home?
Of this, how many were used to clean, dry and iron your clothes?
How many items of clothing did you purchase?
Of these, how many were preloved/second-hand?
How many total clothing items you bought were made from more than 75% recycled or sustainable material?
How many miles did they travel from where they were made to where you purchased them?

How many watt hours were used to power your personal devices?
What source(s) of energy were used?
In gigabytes, how much data did you use cumulatively across work and personal uses?
In kilograms, what was the weight of your general waste collection?
In kilograms, what was the weight of your recycling collection?
In kilograms, what was the total food waste of your home?

How many new or additional plastic bags or single-use plastic products did you use?

In pounds, how much have you donated to charity?
Of this, how much is eligible to be included in this survey
as having a positive impact on the environment?
For guidance, please see Appendix i.iv.

In pounds, what is your total combined credit limit
across all fossil-fuel-invested financial institutions?
To date, how much is invested or saved
in any fossil-fuel-invested financial institutions?
What is your total combined credit limit
across all regenerative-invested financial institutions?
To date, how much is invested or saved
in any regenerative-invested financial institutions?

MYCOREMEDIATION

Mycelium is a body without limits: a body without a plan.
Merlin Sheldrake, *Entangled Life*, Bodley Head, 2020

I want to be a mushroom,
I declare, her front door swinging open
to a clock singing the hour,
announcing dusk's phantom light down the hall.
Come in, she says, surprisingly unsurprised,
I'll put the kettle on.

I continue as I climb the stairs,
It's not that I want to actually become a mushroom...
disappearing into the back room.
She replies inaudibly from the kitchen below
where she is willing the water to boil faster
until a hasty spoon chimes off the rim of a cup.

Returning, I inhale,
only to be held by the unwavering rudder of a single,
stoic finger until she is settled,
cup on the table, glasses in position,
notebook in hand.
A steadying breath,
eye contact,
an invitation.

I've calcified, you see,
into a big, solid, stranded, stationary piece of stone,
and I want to stick my head in the ground,
allow something subterranean and full of tendrils
to crawl into each orifice,
to crowd my ear canals and muffle the tinny hum of self;
to peek out from eyelids and filter green from grey;
hang from nostrils to mask the scent of petrol;
to erode the stranglehold of my forehead
and break the padlock of my jaw;
rouse the flaccid tongue lying beached in my mouth.

The end of her pen dervishes in wild spirals and loops,
its tip counting the steady steps of each word to the page.
How do I queer my neurolinguistic programme,
reconfigure the distorted atlas colonists claimed was self-portrait,
become a body without a plan?
She lowers her pen, emptied quicker than expected,
and swiftly, between words, replaces it with another,
smooth as ballet.

Help me decentralise the nervous system,
dethrone the monarchy of the skull,
assassinate the autocrat of the default mode network.
Give way for the anarchy of the heart, the democracy of gut,
those urgencies abandoned and overgrown.
If I can sprout in that wilderness,
evidence I'm still connected
to something that can surprise me,
I might recover the unrelenting optimism
of a young boy before the world bruised him.
A flash of fear. She smiles.

I want to give my body out on loan to a fungus,
have it blur vague the borders between atmospheres
and dive dizzy through their torus, ad infinitum,
until I am maddened by the minds
that call me landscape,
until I feel microscopic to my own planet,
until it feels dwarfed by the universe
and I stand astride the miniscule and the massive.
She nods, having long abandoned
any hope of getting something useful out of me today.

Is rotting into healing something we can do here?
Because otherwise I think I'll curdle into coal,
and I'd rather litter pick all that's waiting to decompose
than have my body become an altar
to something that once happened to it.
If I'm going to grieve,
I want to put it to better use.

She exhales, audibly.
I sit in relieved shame.
Scanning her notes,
she turns a page and asks,
How's the same time this day next week?

A CEREMONY FOR BROKEN BARK

Here, black rope sinks, bargaining for balance
inside a maw of swallowing earth.
Pallbearers tend with more thought than prayer to
pour libation,
giving to ground what a grandmother gave first
so that she, in turn,
may bestow what's been given back to green.

When a tree falls in a forest,
it gifts its growth back to the understorey,
hopeful that greedy grubs might flourish,
feasting on the femur of a fallen fir.

Spurred into sharing,
dying nurtures us the same
with the scent of pine after rain,
by matching cups of tea, again and again,
the threatening sting of a wooden spoon.
They will be scarce soon, these stories, these trees,
if we let them leak from memory.

Instead of elegy, apology or a buried goodbye,
can the past become a pit for planting?
Held in the hollow of language,
the mine of a mouth,
the gawp of a glass tipped to toast,
could the soil become a womb
where the bulbs of our bodies eventually bloom?

Here, the only chapel where I pray freely
stands with you soaked into its memory.
Finds me
looking for a place to grieve
and calls my eyes
towards its leaves.

BIOPHONY

i

Someone stares so long
they forget their face in the mirror.
Features sit in a demented and vulnerable want,
just angles, all significance replaced,
memory swapped for mystery,
and, unsure if this twinned unknowing
scares or comforts them, they ask aloud,
trying to decipher which side of the glass they stand,
Whose face is that?

ii

A fraught bibliosomniac retreats
from the dread-mist forming beyond the duvet.
Worrying they're reading too much into reading,
they begin to consider language might be
in itself
a poem, a symphony, a cliché, an abbreviation,
an heirloom of hiddenness,
an overdose of nuance,
the revolution of a new colour,
but wonders how
and falls down a rabbit hole of fractals
where sleep catches them before they hit the bottom.

iii

I stand in an old forest and listen
to the wind billow the sails of the canopy,
leaves thrashing a thousand tiny fists.
It sounds like it ought to mean something,
an inhalation before a sermon,
but it's just the orchestra of the world
where each note is a jailer's key
taunting our deadlocked senses
to open in a tender tearing
till it sorts cack-handed cacophony
from sonorous song,
susses sequence from story.

COLLECTIVE BODY, FLESH OF THE EARTH

after Jess Arndt

I want a body that *we* can live in,
with earthen muscle and fungal synapse.
I want an unborderable body.
I want a body that cannot be capitalised upon
nor domesticated into agriculture.
I want a body that speaks kindly
even when the truth is cruel.
I want a body with landscape for organs
that pumps photosynthetic,
that couldn't cross a tipping point
even if it wanted to.

I want a green body.
I want a body that isn't afraid
to recognise itself in volcanoes and storms,
that plays beautiful music
on the finely tuned strings of its ecology.
I want a body that challenges what it means to love
and be loved,
that displays a million different ways of it
until we laugh at the smallness of what we had before.

I want a body solid as a tectonic plate
that people would gather and legislate for.
I want a body beyond sustainable,
an organic, free-range, old-growth body.
An unmineable body.
I want a body that fruits whatever I need
when I need it.

A body with no waste, no spoil or burden.
A bodyscape that makes poets write
about the homes they can never return to.
I want *our* body; the collective body,
flesh of the earth.
I want a body with a future long enough
for it to die of natural causes.

THE WAITING OF THE ROOD

Standing inside the crooked majesty of his crown,
he towers over me, wide as he is tall.
I follow each limb, meandering like a rivulet,
towards a hundred palms outstretched towards the sun,
as if he were expecting some sort of recompense
for his presence.

Ancient lightning forks through the middle of his torso;
he holds himself in two ghost halves
that whisper still across the metre-wide synapse
between left and right.

Time ticks slower around him, calm,
patient, in no rush to go anywhere
having seen how just about everything comes back around
if you can only bear to wait long enough.

> He tells me I haven't waited long enough,
> that I will only be able to hold a wound like his
> when I have waited long enough,
> but I don't know if that means
> that I'm waiting *towards* something
> or *away* from it.

He creaks without moving, the work of being solid
enough to elicit the faintest moan of strain,
and I feel the knots in my body slip out of their bondage,
am somehow taller for just sitting here,
waiting.

MIMOSA PUDICA

*Also called touch-me-not, this evergreen perennial is
sensitive to the touch.*

Waxy leaves sit like plumage
in a careful, perfect stagger.
A finger moves along the stem
like the soft curve of a lover's shoulder.
I watch the leaves collect themselves,
folding in retreat:
a polite but certain refusal.

Touch-shy, I yearn for it to unclench
and teach me the mechanics of letting go,
how it comes to trust the curling is a caress
and not the finger round a trigger.

We both want the velvet touch of sky,
to sense ourselves being felt back
in the soft collision of presence
and for the light to run through us
like it's supposed to.

THE WILDERNESS OF SORROW

The wilderness of sorrow
makes us feral in our grief.
We beg, steal and borrow
whatever brings relief.

The heart might become abandoned bracken,
demanding a barbed embrace,
but we must remember that the tempt of blossoms
is what brought us to this place.

Map its untamed heaviness
and learn to read the land;
it won't always be so painful,
nor will it always be this sad.

Explore and it will start to form
a place, of sorts, where each seed lies,
and in the mess of the life there that lives
we begin to cultivate our lives.

SPRING IS A CALCULATION OF SAFETY

Stirred by the calculable arrival of the sun,
I wake, long slept and dream-weary,
from a hibernation too deep to measure.
Instinct uncurls me from the confines of seed
and a tender limb slips from its casing.

I remember the cold, wet, mulchy scent of self
that hangs like a thread,
a tether dropped from a ladder through the dirt,
the sunshine whispering all that waits for me above,
that spring is a calculation of safety.

I remember being bark and branch, being solid,
opening my lungs to the sun
and throwing my veins out into the atmosphere.
I know the world will try to strip me bare when I get there,
but that's no surprise.
There's beauty in how we survive,
the flourish of the struggle;
an energy that keeps the cycle turning.

CIANALAS

i

Another back-broken dawn lifted through the house,
roused from rest those who secured that light
from whatever yesterday could offer.
Before the eyes opened, the heart tugged
like the boat tethered down in the harbour.
Yanked, again and again,
by the ghosts of all who left
across that many-swallowed sea,
calling for a time of assurance
in the providence of days,
for more rest than this momentary phase
between those stern and steady waves.
Each of their ground, hungry days
petitioned the next for a little bit more ease.

ii

Trifolded letters sit like abandoned proclamations,
ready for when there's more bandwidth to open them,
but before then, the subconscious precursor
of everything being driven by the cost of everything else
scrawls an agile, imperfect formula in the mind,
the scales of utility and value,
but I must not have worked it out correctly
because all that's left is lack.
That can't be right, surely? the heart chugs,
like an old bus pulling out of the station:
slow, steady, but in desperate need of repair.

iii

Those same hearts will fracture but not quite break,
like a spiderwebbed, neon screen,
pixels bleeding through each crack.
This will be the cost of it all,
this schism of self-made scarcity,
of people filled with the burn to return somewhen easier,
somewhere a little less violent
than empty shelves and red weather warnings.

iv

What will there be to say about the future
imperfect, except for that its longing
will make any cavity into a cave, a shelter, a shield,
and we'll live inside everything we'll fail to achieve?
If we are to be left salvaging from the past
to pave the path of a future's future,
can today courier each clod from one day into the next,
as good as yesterday, healthier if we can safely manage it?
Because when it asks if I am being a good ancestor
I say, *I've tried, I'm trying, I will try,*
in a steady wave, as if pulling my heart from its docks,
that land-lust calling me towards something
I might have already lost.

v

I'm homesick for a calmness,
like a spirit itching to arrive and stretch its legs
in the leisure of a landing's windless balance.
It pulls me like a tide to an indiscernible deep,
guiding with a memory of having gone this way before.
I cannot think in its direction,
can only sense myself to its shore.
It is a place I must feel my way to then,
rowed with the steady beat of hope
towards that indeterminate lodestar,
bringing home to it
the other half of its wandering heart.

PERIODICAL CICADA

Is it normal to be scared,
even though I know this will be good for me?
Somewhere else pubs soak punters in malt and light,
cats idle about untroubled streets,
but today I am here, adjacent to all that.

You know, I read about cicadas the other day, she says,
how they burrow underground
for something like seventeen years.
They've calculated the life cycle of their predators
and have hopscotched around those patterns
so that they'll emerge when it's safer for them.

Must be hard being down there
in the dark for so long, I reply,
taking the bait.

We do what we can to protect ourselves,
though some might seem more extreme than others.
She tucks a lock of hair behind her ears,
a signal I have learned is a fighting stance.
Does yours feel this extreme?
I offer a resigned, throaty chuckle in surrender,
caught in the headlights of her reflected glasses.

Coping mechanisms are designed
to be abandoned eventually,
and I know the noise of life
can be overwhelming and intimidating,
but you're here because you can feel it,
that other body beneath your skin, that animal,
island blue and phantom white,
gnawing from the inside out.

It knows it's safe, that it's time,
but this outer you, this exoskeleton
prioritises safety over living
because the facts are

life is scary
and every day is a risk,
but what you need to remember
is that life itself is nothing
compared to being too scared to live at all.

DIALECT

The world writes itself. It can read and be read.
Katie Holten, 'Stone Alphabet', *Emergence Magazine*,
8 May 2019

It is constantly speaking,
a pulse of grammar
threaded through ecology.
A syntax felt in how water
falls across the windshield.
Verbs find themselves tested
against time
in the slow erosion of a coast.

It is a long language,
but, having barely started forming,
we must be patient in our listening;
see the elaborate nuance
in a hummingbird landing to feed;
find the specific tone of lichen
gradually wearing a boulder into dust;
enjoy the sarcasm of a wood pigeon's dawn chorus.

We are limited in our senses,
unable to monologue the migration of magnetic fields,
see the dazzling subtext in ultraviolet eyes
or hear shapes build edges in our ears.

Diverged, our dialect lost its sense to the world around us,
its words pointing only back at ourselves,
mouths modelled from our minds.
We have no need for nature now,
for we can build worlds without it.

Violence blooms in our blind spots then,
tongues releasing terror into the ear of the world,
until, shrinking in our ignorance,
mouths hollow like mute caves
and we can speak of nothing else.

TRACKS

This sky is always grey paper here,
scratch-marked with muddy stones
picked from the bottom of my shoe.
September branches reach like witches' hands
pinching the clouds to burst again.
Dotted moss green and wet brown
     – a frog of a day.

Even the seagulls surrender
and moor in momentary lakes
moulded into dips in the field.
It rained like a trickle of mist at first,
then fat slurps even the canopy couldn't keep
from falling from its chin.

Returning summons, marks memories
at first porous to the other,
     pouring as Sunday afternoon does to evening,
     as solstice stirs to equinox,
     as belonging blends to place,
until we erode into ourselves a path,
like the same song played over and over,
unprepared for how much these familiar routes will feel like lies
when we start to walk off their beaten track.

SHOPPING FOR MUSHROOMS

for L

Mam goes shopping for mushrooms,
stalking fluorescent aisles for
the sprouts of stems and caps.
Prodding through plastic wrap
for the fattest, widest and most wild,
hoping these fruits of connection might lend you their tether,
might call your cells home
      from their wayward wandering.
Again.

Steam escapes from beneath pot lids,
smudging with the sounds of Wimbledon in the air around us;
tints the windows as, outside,
spring washes the world ready for summer.

Squeezing flecked, grey ambrosia,
her hands remind the forest tonic of its nature,
the kind power of mutualism
in this ritual named *what-else-can-I-do*.

Mam makes soup with mushrooms,
cream, a hint of pepper
and enough salt to chap your tongue,
and we shout at the umpires
until the emptied bowls go cold.

FÉILEACÁN

*Féileacán is the Irish word for butterfly. Féile in Irish means
festival or celebration – though the words may not be
etymologically related.*

The city bustles beneath me.
Resting on a bench looking down,
it becomes all myth, drama and chaos
simply passing by.
I notice a chubby green and yellow caterpillar
mistaking my jacket for a flower and, curious,
lift him with a gentle finger,
see he is as full as a thing that small could be.
>I wonder if he feels the pull of it at all
>or if he's content with the task at hand.
>Does he fear the finality of that silk chrysalis coffin
>and what comes after?
>Could he ever know that he'll return
>from that annihilation
>iridescent in a new expression?

This shrub is his country, this park his planet,
this city a universe sprawling out beyond his care,
so is it possible that he can anticipate the journey he's about to make,
the magnitude of those crossed borders
spanning the breadth of broad continents?
Will he enjoy a smug flicker of freedom as he passes us by
or does he feel burdened
that his life is a baton to be passed on?
Do you think he'd be angry at us,
wasting the preciousness of time we're given,
dragging ourselves across the gaps between days on a calendar,
burying ourselves in circumstance?
If we knew we had less time than we have,
what would we want our lives to be?

I'm waiting for something down there
to give me permission
to climb out of the galloping river of life
and ease into a babbling brook,
but he has no need to be anything
other than what he is now;
he is as good a creature as he needs to be
to become celebrated with flight later.

Are we not deserving
of such permission ourselves,
to find some rest
amidst the drama of our lives?

THAW

Action is the best antidote to despair
James Bradley, 'UNEARTHED', *Meanjin*, spring 2019

I open my mouth
to explain how my mind is a catching engine,
but instead, without ceremony or introduction,
a glacier falls straight out of my throat,
just sits there, stubbornly melting
in the middle of my counsellor's box room.

Her pursed lips loosen, eyebrows rise like a tide
and, pointing with the tip of her pen,
she suggests I hold it like an inner child,
so I lean in from the fold-out sofa bed
with the kind of tentative hug
you'd give at an office party you weren't invited to,
and turn my face from its dripping shimmer.

Clocks continue to tick deadlines on both walls,
counting twice the time along a rising shoreline
that passes marks of a child's growth
notched into the doorframe
reading *Venice, Amsterdam, London, New York.*
We laugh about nineties disaster movies
like we aren't already in one.

Her smile quivers like an exhaust pipe
and I wonder if counsellors get CPD for stuff like this.
How safe can she make this space, really?
Is it triggering to know
it's not just the world inside my head that's on fire anymore?
Can she hear the whipping permafrost crack,
gunslinging from across the room as well?
Does she smell the same billowing popping candy
of forest fires snap from downstairs?
Is she woken to the harmonium drone
of bulldozers marching in the streets,
echoing like tinnitus?

I wipe the ice with my sleeve to clear a window through the frost
and see inside little plastic figurine people:
a diorama of a future suspended in suffering,
frozen in a potential perpetual apocalypse,
a momentary monument to inaction.
They will move only when enough of it melts,
while we wait for urgency to free us from distraction.

I ask across the shimmering, blue horizon,
where cups clink off floating icebergs,
Which do you think will thaw first?
The metaphor, or the ice itself?

SEEDS OF METHUSELAH

Fallen into fable,
we cried through the rubble,
begged for careful hands to care us back to colour.
Watched the world forget us
as we held on to the unbegun sprout
of our long-lived leaves.

Here, in the cage of our coats,
we learned the difference between
being buried and being planted.

It was only in our recovery
that we found our fruit again,
remembered the medicine in our bark.
We grow now as natural and native,
like we'd never been lost in the first place.

Nothing worth nourishing
loses its place for long;
our souls are as minerals
in the soil of the world,
so if you find yourself lost,
as we once were,
learn to put yourself in the hands
of someone who knows
what it is
you need to grow.

DETRITIVORE

Imagine if every leaf that ever fell
instead of decomposing just lay around,
solid as the day it dropped.

Wouldn't we drown in the ghosts of gone summers
as they clogged up our streets?
Wouldn't our houses creak under the weight of them;
wouldn't they block every door?
Wouldn't these skeletons of dead light
plunge us into darkness under such impossible weight?

Love the millipedes, then;
praise the woodlice and blowflies.
Cherish the termites and cockroaches;
yes, hail to all the earthworms and snails!
The detritivores that free us
from the insurmountable discard of seasons,
that jailbreak the hidden food in grounded leaves
and feed us through the soil.

Isn't the point of all that passes
simply to go
and gift us with the richness of memory instead?
Strange, then, mustn't it seem
for important work to have such ugly labour,
but how like us they are,
our own ugly work just as helpful
when we toil our own way through
everything that's fallen
and can no longer serve its purpose.

LESSONS IN LIMBO

Sefton Park is a daffodil tonic.
French bulldogs roll in its yellow.
Pensioners eat homemade sandwiches by the boating lake
and I rest my spine up along the trunk of a tree.

This is who we are when the shops are closed,
when the pubs haven't opened,
when the city doesn't call us;
Church Street is an empty photo now
and the docks remember their long-suffered silence.

There is a billion pound more food in our homes
than three weeks ago,
and I can't help but feel like something's rotten.
The city might be shut down,
but I feel like I'm just beginning to open
now that I've seen how quickly we can change
when we are forced.

BEHAVIOUR

A wooden buddha roosts on the bookshelf,
mouth melting into a knowing smile
as he supervises her stenography of my madness.
I scan the titles beside him,
frantic for clues.

I've been fading more and more
since we've started talking about behaviour;
a flicker here, a flash from time to time.
By now she's struggling to find eye contact at all.
I see her searching for an approximate position,
careful to remain calm
when all she sees
is a cream wall behind me.

You know there's a frog in the Arctic circle
that freezes its blood to survive the winter?

She nods, knowing I communicate in pilgrimages.

Or do you ever think about giraffe necks?
How generations reaching for leafier branches
finally gave them the lift they needed?

Wood pigeons coo their suburban patter,
tarmac melts through the window,
tailgating a lazy breeze.

What does this feel like in your body?
She encourages a more direct path.
Like a need to stretch.
Like this is someone else's skin.

Like I'm lonely for myself.

The words hang there
as if dappled from the trees outside;
a twinkle of a wind chime,
a car door flashing as it closes in the sun.

What would it feel like, she daydreams to the ceiling,
if you could harness everything it takes to disappear
and direct it into something
that would make you feel more solid,
more alive, more yourself?

I think of colour-changing cuttlefish,
dung beetles charting paths of celestial light,
lizards dropping limbs like disposable prosthetics,
and bowfin fish fixing eyes to their tails.

To have that much choice
would feel like forgiveness.

Just then, a lightless dawn turns between the walls.
Faintly, she finds my gaze.
I have, at least, a semblance of an edge
as if I were made of hot, blown glass.

Shuffling, I shimmer a glittered phantom
to frame the god perched over her shoulder.

ADVICE FROM THE ELEMENTS

Do you think I wake each morning with the rising sun asking where I'm up to with the growing since the morning previous? Do you think the wind rattles through me, whispering all the reasons why I'll fail? Do you think I sleep fitfully, fearing the time lost to rest? Do I worry about holding enough space for birds nesting in my canopies? Do you think I feel grounded in the moment, rooted in mindfulness for the dirt beneath my foundations? Do you think I'm anxious over targets, deadlines, cash flows and impact? Do you think I worry I'm developing a sunlight dependency, finding myself contorting into strange, knotted shapes to reach it? Do I feel all the insects crawling on my skin, like a paranoid sickness?

No. I am a tree. It is in my nature to be so.

Do you think I worry that, yes, I'm flowing, but how's my form? Do you think I need more time to settle in? Do I pine for the great heights of my mountain source? Am I reckless in this race, not stopping to take in the sights? Do you think I'm unable to stop and relax? Do you wonder what I'm chasing after, or what I'm running from? Do you think I feel the corruption of concrete, corporate pipes? Do you think I feel like the *right* river, that I wish I'd taken a different route? Do I turn pebbles over at night, drowning in the despair of a wrong decision? Do you think I fear my death in the ocean? Do you think I cling to bedrock, dragged against the course, worrying if I should surrender to its force or not? Do you think I feel alone, separated from my sibling tributaries gone to flow by themselves?

No. I am a river. It is my nature to be so.

Do you think I feel represented and understood? Do I feel really seen? Do you think I struggle to take up space? Am I haunted by abandon, my work never really being appreciated: the seed spreading, the cloud commuting, the moisture magician, the essential breath – do you think I value my zephyr? Am I frustrated with how you make me music; do I feel mocked? Do you think I'm tired of always being what holds everything else together, working in the negative spaces? Do I feel silenced? Do I explode into hurricanes and tornadoes, do I rage just to feel real? Do I self-harm? Consumed by self-destructive properties, do I feel used and undervalued, having carried your songs without thanks for your breath? Just the middleman, exchanging and negotiating magic on your behalf? Do I just want to let off some steam; am I desperate to feel myself in a real body, not this flimsy, untethered thing? Do you worry if I've ever felt appreciated? Do I wander through cracked open windows and ajar doors just to feel hollowed out by life?

No. I am the air. It is simply my nature to be so.

Do I want a little bit of something back? Do I think of just moving to a more appreciative cluster of planets? The whole system revolves around me, but do I feel you're grateful for this? Do I crave the tactile, lonely in my intensity? Would that make me introverted or extroverted? Distanced because I need to be, or shining outward because I can't bear to be alone? Do I know how to practise self-care, having literally been burning the candle of your planet at both ends? Do I dream of a holiday? Do I feel pressure to provide? Do I understand my responsibility as your wholly dependent provider, or does it just feel like too much? What do I do for fun? Am I slightly disturbed by the things I've cast my light on? How do I keep my cool? Am I a militant disciplinarian or more progressive? Do I fear an inner darkness, hence all this outward show of light? Do I feel that furnace in myself raging? Am I able to appreciate my work, the lush green brushstrokes here and the azure watercolour there painted on the canvas, or do I see it as an interference? Do I have your attention, or are you so concerned with the comfort of the day that you're just worried about staying out of the dark?

No. I am the sun. It is just my nature to be so and nothing more.

BREATH IS A SPIRIT WE SHARE

Held in the soft spot where we meet the world,
these breaths are expensive:
each lungful a membrane, a fontanelle, a stoma,
each exchange a gift, a grave and a gavel.
For every white dove we exhale
we ground another on the in
when power seeks a supple neck
on which to rest its knee.

It is the tax we pay the trees
to keep them sleeping,
blowing wispy tributes to their canopies,
hopeful their jewelled foliage will not waken,
nor their barked bodies uproot themselves to reclaim the earth.

Before there was a word
there was the breath with which to make it,
its free flow so sacrosanct
that to chain a vowel in writing
is considered sin,
so we illustrate the air
in the playful ways we hold,
twist and bend it,
building languages with perversions
of the most unspeakably holy.

It is the key to the locked door of this body,
anchors my soul in it long enough to call it home,
opens the curtains but is wary of the windows
in case it should slip out and vanish once again.

Breath is a spirit we share;
our constant substance
returns us over and over
to that relationship of living.

TRACE FOSSIL

A trace fossil is a bracing of space by a vanished body, in
which absence serves as sign.
        Robert Macfarlane, *Underland*, Hamish Hamilton, 2019

The evening is a dark marble bowl
encased over the sky.
Cars trace neon lights
like a city's vital signs.
Shopfronts cast pavements in
operatic incandescence
and the lamps in this little room
paint shadowed garden leaves ashen grey,
though it probably looks cosy from outside.

We are investigating a trace fossil,
mining narrative in its negative space;
a story extant only in impressions.
It's funny how gentle it looks after all this time.
A fox shrieks across the sentry of bins along the alley.
She clasps a button at her cuff.
I wipe green tea from my lip.
It feels as though I miss it, but I don't.

She squints a fraction, adjusting her focus.
I continue:
Healing is a kind of loss, but the heart,
well, that can take a little longer to let go,
but this, this is not a record; it's a mould.
I see the creature that crawled out of this shape.
In this, I see what I escaped.

INCENTIVISING FALLING TO THE DEADWEIGHT

Their tongue is buried beneath this mountain;
unable to lift and unbury their speaking,
they walk instead towards the summit
as if it were a dictionary
eroded out from the ground:
a landsculpt of elevation
puncturing the yolk of the day.

Ascending,
with each step a nerve is plucked
from the soles of planted feet
and laid gently down on the rock,
which learns it wasn't a misplaced mouth
but a heart so close to exploding
that if they gave it breath
it'd blow into a sinew-splattered
sweep of branches,
veins having burst into wings.
Proof, maybe, that a world this harsh
can turn you inside out after all.

The climb shows the beauty
in each dutiful ache of its skyward stretch:
how it incentivises falling to its deadweight,
how the wind will hoist your unburdened hands
towards the mumbling muse of a sky overhead
where clouds like inkwells
wait for the tips of fingers
to swell and sway like leaves,
writing cursive with every passing breeze.

There, questions move like an umbilical shoot,
sprouting in pursuit of light,
and little by little, day after day,
chlorophyll question marks bend,
clear and intentional
as a leaf opening to the sun,
and each thought becomes oxygen

ABSCISSION

Autumn is an auburn flirt,
tipsy on just one more for the road,
unaware that the path's been growing
darker by the day,
shortened as light retreats along.

Soon we'll come to the end,
treading tides of spent leaves,
watching the wind whisper the edges of embers overhead
until they fall from their rubied crowns in pink clouds.

> We've been here before,
> although then it was midnight,
> cosy in your garden,
> drunk on the wishes of comets
> before they were snuffed from the sky
> like birthday candles.
> We saw them shooting when they were falling,
> but now we are heavy with slipping
> when we feel we ought to be flying.

The branches know they have two choices:
they can either let go or be dragged,
and while it's not quite mourning for us,
still, we grieve;
we have to
if we're to be unburdened
from the expectation of being evergreen.

It won't feel kind or good,
but necessity seldom does.
Even when it comes to hurt a little less,
that in itself will sting
like a sharp-edged stone in our shoes
wading through the fallen stars on this shrunken path,
reminding me how this release
promises better buds in spring.

SOLASTALGIA

Distracted and disassociated eyes
trace the maps' coastlines,
wondering where each line falls
between verbatim and memoir.

It feels like an insidious slipping, I tell her,
never steep enough to feel the need to correct myself;
it just gets harder to stand upright each day.

Clearing myself of it feels too much
like filibustering inside an airlocked room;
that I'm pulping old growth to write policy or poetry on,
only to burn the book
to get enough light to read it by.

Shifting, the white quiff of Greenland balds,
freckles of islands disappear,
the continents' cheeks go gaunt
and peninsulas snap like broken teeth.

We are living in the pathology
of mistaking the gifts of the world
for what we feel entitled to,
so your reaction,
however damaging,
is quite reasonable. I'd say
your grief is correct.

Like a backwards sympathetic magic,
some pathetic fallacy in reverse –
how else could you witness such collapse
without becoming testament to it?

The problem is
we usually grieve when we are bereft,
when the thing we love has up and left,
but now what should be lost remains
only changed, keeps changing,
completely and in unrecognisable ways.

My heart palpitates,
earthquakes ripple through the canvas.
My nerves boil into bitumen,
muscles desertify into dust.

What if you treated this like any other death,
a bodily event, something to put into a casket,
one big enough to catch every charred flake from the forest fires,
every orphaned glacier that calved into the sea,
and closed the lid shut?

Would that give you your body back?
You can't hold all of that in there,
you are not a sovereign to a dying world,
you do not need to suffer twice over.

What if
you made a poem like a coffin
and buried it?

OVERBURDEN

It's quiet, save the percussive rain on the window.
Stillness holds us here
where I sit   at a distance
buried beneath a landfill of anger
at how
to become it
we must first *unearth*
and how little I have to show
for all this digging.

She worries the trim of my stoicism
with a concerned, gentle hum.
Today, you want to give in to it, right?
Pinching the bridge of her nose,
she blinks, resting her glasses on the table
before clapping closed the notebook.
Its solitary thud is hefty
with all the ink inside.
I shift unconsciously in my seat.

I can see the knuckles of your mind
breaking through its skin,
how you've ground your teeth to dust.
I know the fury it takes to survive sometimes,
the spite, the stubbornness.

She holds my gaze for longer than I'd like.
But if you think you've been excavating,
you haven't even touched a shovel yet.
What we've been doing is plotting how to detonate,
and I know it seems you're being crushed,
but so was coal before it came into its value.
When you feel like you're starting to crack,
remember that every seed
has that same sinking feeling
before it taps root.

She smiles, pained and sympathetic.
It would be impossible to heal
if you didn't feel even just a little bit broken at first
and, while I can't promise this won't hurt less,
it will clear some space,
allow us to find a vein of truth
like a seam of gold
that we'll follow
together
towards the centre.

I slump like slagheap,
surprised to hear
we've both been writing poetry
and how I am redrafted
with each of her mysterious pages,
each verbatim catharsis becoming
the stanzas of a man.

That sounds nice, I say,
think that would be good,
and smile, tired but undefeated,
understanding that this is how
we are like poems ourselves:
never finished,
just abandoned.

BODY AS COLONY

The heart is a claimed and plundered castle.
When this flag is finished burning,
they will mast a new one in its place.

Statues stand as stories,
reminding us what happened here
until we forget what shape the hills were before.

It comes like a new organ resisting rejection;
placated nerves crawl into remodelled infrastructure,
better to accommodate the change
until its reflex becomes policy
and returning to before turns impossible.

I pay my tribute in pounds of blood,
squeezing full each one
until I am an arid field of once-was.
The vast expanse of my forgiveness
is a prairie to be tilled and ploughed,
suckled of all kindness
so that others may feed first.

The deeds to my body are signed in a foreign script,
its crimes tried in an unspeakable tongue
by laws I neither recognise nor support.

Coups are quelled, families bicker
as neat lines divide me into smaller and smaller plots,
fracturing any sense of semblance,
any suggestion of being the same.

At night I dream myself untouched,
see the streets roar in raucous indigeneity,
the threshold of spirit never destroyed,
the body having never been someone else's.

GEOPHAGY

When I was split from the soil,
uprooted and torn from my other body,
the land became different;
agency gone, it now, suddenly, *belonged*,
no longer its own viceroy or king.

Harvested like a crop,
upside down till all the blood pooled
and I was told to forget what I knew:
that the soil was an ancestor of mine,
that my own fed it with their flesh,
that it was a long-promised home
I could return to.

Two pits, then, were left behind
where they plucked me:
one in the earth and another
in the landmass I had become.
Bones built themselves
around a deep and cavernous want
that I've been trying to fill in
like the outline of a forgotten child,
sketching only silhouette, the absence of form,
a placeholder for a person,
because our grief doesn't lessen;
we grow around it
until it becomes harder and harder to find.

This hunger is a proclamation,
a symptom of lacking,
a sign that I took my kidnapper's last name.
Look at me, striding around
in their one-two steps
like this is how I've always walked.

I want this roughage to scour me clean of
who they said I was,
remind each tiny cell of the taste of itself
and feed myself
until I break the back of this need.

I hold the terrain in my hand like fruit,
turn its glistening mulch in the sun,
speckled and shiny.
This is the root of my starvation:
that the magic mixed through this soil
lives outside me now.

Clod-craving, earth eater,
tell me this hunger is normal.
Tell me it is okay to want this
because I can't bear to learn
there might be another way.
My mouth has been a hollow,
open grave so for long;
please, tell me you can fill it in.

UNSAIN

Nestling in lazy beds
braided along the hills,
I weep;
nourish the soil
in the wet of our disconnect.

My body knows
what it never learned,
a sensation of tearing
as the stories of ourselves
slip away.

Salted at the root,
we were piled up in pits
as if the only penance
could be our bodies.

Meeting abandon with abandon,
we've been passing down these empty bowls,
whispering to never let our children starve again.

I'll wring out of myself
an antidote to holy water,
unsain the landscape
back into multiplicity and myth,
show it that I'm here now,
apologising for not understanding earlier
how it was a kidnapping.

OGHAM

Held by the flimsy spine of inheritance,
I graft myself, patiently learning
that my body grows what I nourish
and returns what I weed
until it is stable enough for me to climb,
babbling like a baby,
and move my mouth around the shapes of the world:
    curving the vowels of lakes,
    solving the sibilance of rivers,
    testing birdsong titters on the backs of teeth,
    ploughing plosives in mast year droppings,
    droning hollows inside thrummed caves.

Each branching word sprouts leaves from its tips,
unfurling to catch sunlight
and stir its sugary magic of understanding
through my illuminated blood.

Swelling, the lexicon spirals stories
through my heartwood like ballast,
permitting play amidst the canopy,
swaying and queered in the mesh of crowns
where language speaks in listening,
diffusing sense into the air like oxygen,
scent-wafting tannins and pine,
the aroma of mulch and rank,
waiting for a blurry body to inhale,
taste the belonging of language
and understand that this blank, bark dictionary
holds more meaning than we could ever say.

TATTIE HOCKED

*From the late 19th century until the late 1980s, a significant
portion of the potato crop in south-western and central
Scotland was harvested by migratory workers from the west
of Ireland. These 'tattie howkers' (or 'hokers') formed a distinct
migrant group and worked in 'squads' of twenty to thirty
members.*

Heather Holmes, 'Irish migratory potato workers in
Scotland: Radharc's "The Tattie Howkers" and its making',
Saothar 26, 2001

i

Piled cards unstack. We steal our spoils
from each other's hands,
sucking laughter down our bellies.
Her grin gleans from behind a palm,
retreating from his ear.
Whispers hiss themselves between teeth,
chasing chardonnay slosh and malice.

ii

Holly Willoughby emerges from the tank, coiffured dry.
A Maris Piper jumps from the bullseye
across the studio into Keith Lemon's hand.
His catchphrase escaping through the rowdy audience
hides itself behind his lips
while they settle into stillness.

iii

A million roads curl up out of the ground;
buildings drop in careful dissolve.
Boats zip a foamy seam,
repairing tears in the water
as the last train to Achill is pulled back to a bothy
by ten sisters who scream themselves to sleep
and dream of starving children
nursed by refluxed coddle
that unboils into ingredients,
a mould left shrinking
from their freckled, peeled skins.

iv

The Empire's stores empty, each eager,
healthy bushel traded for a brave English boy
marching backwards into his mother's arms,
who unstitches buttons to dangle like ripe fruit
from crimson coats that have been bleeding trails
back into the bodies of other mothers' sons that,
only last week, lay beneath their boots.

v

Our deck is reassembled and interred into its box.
Each invasion reverses,
leaving the ghosts peering over her shoulder
waiting to solidify into graves that were never dug.

THE WORD FOR LANGUAGE IS TONGUE

... we also learned that there is no verb 'to have' in Welsh, in the sense of 'to possess'. Things, people, accidents, headaches, houses, even, are only 'with you', as if by their consent.

Pamela Petro, *The Long Field*, Little Toller, 2021

To make it a verb
is to indistinguish action from act.
Impossible, then, to think one could exist
without the other
when voice is the fuel on which
the engine of meaning is sparked.

A temporary thing,
only ever present then gone:
how a breeze becomes a breath
becomes a breeze again –
a lexicon living in the rippling river,
the turn of an auroch's head,
the sway of fresh grass
and how monkeys hang their tails in serifs.

We spoke one pulse at a time
until writing estranged us
from the orchestra of mingling presences,
muted us in the loneliness of our mouths,
a cage for words
where we stashed everything we thought to name
until, crawling out of ourselves,
holding clods of dirt in our fists
and forcing one wisdom into another,
we spoke only of dominion.

We've gone around
cutting the world up into words ever since,
seizing as we speak by rote,
slackening our mouths against nuance,
no longer muscles of perception

but judgement, deeming all that seems inanimate
not just dead but having never been alive.

We no longer pat down the earth with a careful tongue,
no longer feel the ritual of becoming,
that unlayering understanding:
the ex-stasis of speech
where each word is a promise to the earth
held close in our hearts,
tethering us to a breathing beast.

KEENING

I pick all the batteries out from the clock in my skull,
roll my wooden-ringed eyes closed along their curtain poles,
turn my mirrored palms over,
swinging whatever light remains across the room
to darken against the wall of my chest,
where, purring gently, that cliff-edged,
tidal throat-swell just before crying
tunes the air, listens for what resonates back,
pats down its invisible presence,
ascertains the shape.
This may be a funeral without a corpse
but that doesn't mean we have nothing to bury.

Time moves differently inside a grieving heart.
I keep it with a gentle fist against my chest
as if knocking it back into step,
as if waking it from shock,
and, with a soothing, silent swaying,
summon the safety of my first cradling,
a suggestion for that same tenderness now,
as I've come to lay this bundle down.

Mourning melts my meaning into murmurs,
stretches words so far from sense
that I've nothing else to notice but the traction
of breath leaving the body,
like it is instruction for the passing
given in an animal song –
the bugle of a heartsore elk,
a howl from a wallowing wolf,
wails of a harrowed humpback –
which is to think about audience,
which is to see another's shoulder
for when the pall needs bearing.

When the weight is lowered
and we've nothing to necessarily gather for,
can we, in the wake of that passing pain,
leave space enough for us to hold each other?

MEGALITH

It takes decades for the gaze to soften the right way,
for the stone's etchings to reveal themselves
as illustrations of time
in every moment the groove deepened
or the curve curled,
and how those sustained semantics
speak through centuries.
>Imagine having so much future ahead of you
>even the capriciousness of language
>would call for such indelible ink,
>only for its meaning to be forgotten
>before the page was weathered bare.

I envy their solidity,
how so often the rock is, quite literally,
a clock they'd set themselves against
to return here, year after year,
to see a solstice peal,
unaware there would ever be a time
that we would fail to recognise each other.

Is there enough future ahead of me
to become ancient to some future soul;
for these carvings,
kept on thinner tomes,
to have lived long enough
for someone to be there
with enough of their own time
to forget its grammar?

SWEAT CURE

The more I look, the closer I see
that my bones are actually sweathouse bricks.
Laid together with the elbow grease and spit
of someone who, just this morning, died
and can now no longer guide me through the past,
leaving me to make what I can
from both their passings.

Grief isolates you from yourself,
casts you adrift from the nation of your flesh,
but I felt my heart should be alone,
needed to be held in the plunged earth
of an interior dark,
because I knew the silence
would leaven it
into a welcome cavity,
an empty disc,
the resounding moon-face of a barn owl
snatching murmurs from the world outside;
gather them in the chorus of my craters
to become the voice of a kind, old god.

Their song condenses into smoke
and that smoke crystallises into a fire
whose heat is a sweat cure
that kneads my muscles from their knotted unknowing,
the skin a ribbon on the knife-edge of their voice,
curling me towards a heart
left tender to the touch
that sounds now like a shell
echoing the sea.

UNMAP

The map said nothing
about how this flourish of rock
looks like it's curling a coiled hand
towards the blanket of the sky,
as if the magma isn't solid yet
and still stubbornly stretches
against the sink of the waves.

The topography only showed me a way through,
never in.
I'd never have seen
that ever-blurring horizon
if I hadn't stepped through
this keyhole at the edge of the world.

There was absolutely zero in there
about how I'd feel
standing between these basalt trunks,
how their heads bloom like canopies of leaves.
I'd never have heard the sea's foamy song
is a tonal poem of understanding.

The map could never have known
that when I asked the womb of the world
for what it calls itself,
I heard it say my name.

CICATRIX

Cut me
and I'll make language.
See the etchings stride with a soldier's conviction,
and bandaged just the same.
Once more unto meaning, dear friends,
once more an urged narration
of the blade deepening after it was removed.

I've heard it is the oldest magic,
that the first word was a wound and
every story is a scar.
We began by carving,
though the axes come to us now,
called home by the handkerchiefs
we wave to the shore.

We welcome their weary necks
drooling silver-edged tongues to nestle in our ribs
like a broken-winged bird, a stitch, a diaspora,
offering their stifled strength to be melted into coins,
candlesticks, promises.

We suckle the splinters from their sex,
tracing the swollen palpitations of our bark-carved hearts.
A ring to mark the marriage of each year
unfolds our bodies into lined pages.

Speaking from where meaning
was notched from us to begin with,
we peer over into the rift,
the remnants, the cicatrix,
hoping that when wisdom grabs our ankles
it'll lift.

HOLOBIONTS

The room feels like a confession box
when I say,
This body knows how to be an inhalation,
how to pretend it's holding itself together
as it slips into the shape of a stranger's lung,
becoming, as if it had always been, their blood.

She rests her chin on a knuckle,
curling an index finger
around her lips like a question mark.

There are times I don't feel completely myself
even without becoming someone else.
Sometimes I am just a landscape
for this assemblage of biota,
merely a colony of bacterial prairies, viral wetlands,
lakes of archaea and forests of fungi.
I often wonder if the planet thinks of me the same,
if I'm just a layer of a fractal.

I look out the window, see puddles of cloud pass.
A plane emerges from one like a coin falling from a pocket.
If we are one way the universe knows itself,
can I slip into that knowing,
hack that same, soft buckling and disappear into
rather than out of?

She lifts her head to smile over the rim of her glasses.

Can consciousness stretch like a canvas
to be stepped back from
until another scene appears
and another and another?

The landscape morphs into portrait now,
slowly coming into focus
like a self-arranging jigsaw,
like a wiped lens,
like the right prescription.

And if all this were true,
what if I cared for my own environment?
Would it rewire the universe to care for me in return
as if coded through those interdependencies?

However we get there, the sense of arriving
is the quiet work of a job well done;
in it I hope she can hear my gratitude.
Could this be how I give and get back to myself,
through knowing myself
as part of a universal commons
and learning how to make a landscape smile?

ANIMA MUNDI

*Thus, then, in accordance with the likely account, we must
declare that this Cosmos has verily come into existence as
a Living Creature endowed with soul and reason … a Living
Creature, one and visible, containing within itself all the living
creatures which are by nature akin to itself.*

Plato, Timaeus

The heart slips back into place,
sits to attention in my chest
having heard its name,
secret even to me,
called from the eye of a lingering wren,
>from the stoic stag's stare,
>from the butterfly sipping sweat off my skin.

God might have taken himself out of the world,
but he wasn't the only one here.
She remains even now,
holds my tender nerves
between her fingers like beads on a string,
rubs them gently,
praying a pulse back into them.

She spools me back from slack,
grafting those thin threads
onto the beauty that stitches the whole world together,
and if I kneel to the wisdom of all my organs,
I can see that the ghost in my shell
is no longer parallel but facing.

A blooming booms across the web,
wind over a leafy trellis,
animating itself into and out of all things,
beating the same pattern
as my own heart like a code
and in that way one alive thing
recognises another,
a sprouting.

MORNING STAR

Untrodden snow crunches gritty but unsalted.
A magpie blinks frost from its feathers
to fatten on more of the moon,
sat like a curled-up silver salamander,
stark against the morning black.
            It could be midnight if you squinted.

Fog folds up from between trees
and terraced roofs like a chilly breath,
lifting just enough for the morning star
to swing under the arm of the sun
and find me standing stark like a suitor
waiting for a dance.

Feet graze grasses like clothes
strewn to a bedroom floor,
our Fibonacci choreography
traces lotus flowers the colour of hearts in love,
pentagrams repeat themselves in pinecones,
vegetables split for soup,
the vibration of a Spanish guitar.

These mementos tingle like nervousness.
A lipstick-smeared handkerchief,
a sly text, perfume on my neck,
the fading image of her
standing in the doorway of a horizon,
the threshold of atmosphere,
clothes bundled to her chest,
shoes hanging from limp fingers,
putting her index to her lips
and leaving.

TRANSLATING BIRDSONG

In the midst of no man's land,
between the silent trees,
semi-precious bullets chirp past.
Messages in pretty little bottles of air
land, exploding Molotovs in petite symphonies.

There, a relentless whirring, machine-gun rattle
urging itself across the canopy
like a dilapidated printer
churning out windchimes.

An alchemy of aether
that punctuates the nothing
with that first insistence of life,
rolling out from the smallest of breaths
tinged with the haw of song.

A tap-tap-screech crescendoes over hum,
fireworks sound in glistening ripples
painted with hollow bones,
beady eyes and polished beaks.
These are the synapses of the air firing.

There, the reliable, chipper beat of one,
steady as a manuscript brought to life,
forms in me that feeling of a finished book,
enjoyed without having read a word.

SALT MOUTH

The whipping wind roaring through driving rain
and the sunken hum of the depth beneath her
swapped frantically like a chess clock,
counting her journey in its stark metre
through the midnight seas, black as a mine.

She swam past Caligula
sinking rounds into the swell,
slow like hail through the current;
past trolleys and engagement rings,
orphaned crutches and forgotten treasures,
submarines and plastic bags;
past cigarette ends and prescription drugs,
makeup wipes and sandwich wrappers;
past cases for obsolete iPhones;
past pink and blue glitter remnants.

She braced her puckered lips against the brine
until a celestial moan emerged from the dust of the deep,
thick enough it might unhook the stark
full moon from the sky.

She stopped,
treading as sure as she could against the sea.
The size of this voice belittled her;
her whole body,
held inside one word of whale,
felt like something she had forgotten
before she was even born.

MAN OF THE FOREST

Pongo abelii
after Michael Longley

Think of yourself,
just differently shaped:
        a thick drop of juice
        sucked from the mandarin.

Your hair has rewilded.
You shine, all over,
like a distant fire among the palms.

Hands curling to caress
betray both thickness and length.

Your face curves out like a black moon,
leathery folds of rusty skin
running from temple to jaw,
mouth a little longer,
and a soul patch of ginger fuzz
crescents under your lips.
Your nostrils semicolons
squashed into the hollow of your face.

Those eyes are the same, though,
edges swelling
like a brim of warmth
fit to burst
in the deep amber hum of your gaze.
A spit of white,
that glint of awareness
looking back.

A MINISTRY OF BABOONS

Without any obvious signal, each of the baboons sat down on a smooth stone surrounding one of the pools, and for a half an hour (by human reckoning) they sat alone or in small clusters, completely quiet, staring at the waters.
James Bridle, *Ways of Being*, Allen Lane, 2022

We gather on Sunday mornings,
kneel before we sit.
Pews remind us this place is not designed
for any mortal comfort.
A man in long cloth ministers about a saviour's suffering
and the debt our flesh must repay.
Looking, we see him hanging from a cross
pierced by all the wounds faith can leave in a man.
Traipsing stringed beads,
we repent each of our mortal sins,
arriving correct at the foot of an absent god.

They gather around pools
and, without bowing, sit.
Solid rock a reminder of the presence of earth.
Here, it is not a time for sermon
but for the homily of silence.
Looking, they see themselves looking,
glimpsing a soul in their understanding.
In stillness, they trace outlines with red and tiny eyes;
reflections emerge clearer as the water settles.

Eventually both of us stand,
go about our days afterwards,
each with the tender ache
of being alive.

INOSCULATE

You've driven us here
while we've driven each other mad.
The day exhales a frustrated gale across the hills,
twigs and leaves rattling in its force.
The sky is a single cloud
hiding us from any kind of sunny resolution.
I bury hands into pockets;
you boil the air with silence
as the romance of a Sunday in November sours.

You walk off to find your own bit of sky to stare into.
I scan the view for a spark of something,
see only lots of a little
except for the gnarled heft of two trees that,
having been wrapped up in each other's silken, roped embrace,
have grown, quite literally, into each other.

I seethe on one far edge
of a damp, wooden bench;
you return to perch opposite,
placing between us a small, warm cup from the van across.
They're not olive trees, but this is a kind of branch
and, begrudgingly, I sip sweet chocolate,
smile, feel your pulse in my veins
like we've grafted them onto each other's hearts.

Even when we become different species,
we kiss inwards, towards our roots
in a deliberate kindness,
inosculated to each other.

THE NATURE OF LOVE

Love me like a river
slipping through the hands of its banks,
and I'll love you like a tree
struck down the middle by lightning
that decides to keep growing regardless.

Love me like the scree
gathered at the foot of the mountain,
and I'll love you like a moment's perfect breeze
in summer heat.

Love me like a mast year giving,
and I'll love you like a glacier
worth the melt.

Love me like a cactus
holding on to the memory of water,
and I'll love you like birdsong
curling air into invisible semiquavers.

Love me like an honourable harvest,
leave some of me behind,
and I'll love you like a spontaneous geyser,
like a shy tectonic plate

Love me like patches of wild gardens
across a vast, grey city
and I'll love you like worms
that will feed on me when I'm dead.

Love me like a coppiced tree, a manicured lawn,
and I'll love you like the memory of bog,
the patience of an oxbow lake.

Love me with the steadiness of a dam,
the generosity of a waterfall,
and I'll love you like the pull of the moon,
like a crown-shy canopy.

Love me like the gift of early fruit,
with the steadiness of seasons,
and I'll love you like a cog of nature,
the best of life,
its meaning and its reason.

KOMOREBI

Komorebi is a Japanese word made up of the kanji for 'tree', 'shine through' and 'sun'. It describes the way sunlight scatters when it filters through leaves.

Praise be to leaf-dappled light,
its dazzling glint and welcome shadow,
a mist-tinged air serene with relief.

Praise be that the sun perches itself
at such a golden distance
that the geometry would align me
in this hallowed prism of perspective.
The mathematics of the most improbable moments,
proof of the regularity of miracles.

Praise be trees, that silent connective tissue,
wordless envoys whose message is mutual aid,
clanging like muffled church bells
in benediction of the absolute truth of this,
broadcast in each leafy exhale.

Praise be the ancestors
for their gift of seeing green,
that they would fix their eyes to forage so much
each future shrub would erupt into fireworks.

Praise be the wealth
of five hundred and fifty-five nanometres of light,
how its familiarity so fits our bodies
we don't even hold it anymore,
knowing the next wash of light won't be far away.
How, now, the congress of each bloom
is a medicine to our voltage.

Yes, praise be to leaf-dappled light,
to the god it stirs sleeping in my breast,
his unending cauldron,
his harp waiting to harken in the spring.

Praise be the chlorophyll
that douses me in possibility,
waiting for a spark to catch
and ignite me in meaning.
Praise be that arboreal ambrosia,
fizzing me in memory.

Praise be the leaves,
so eager to applaud us in the passing breeze,
catching us in their limed light,
reminding us of who we are.

Yes, praise be today and this moment,
the reward in and of itself to be here,
speckled in this leaf-dappled light.

QUEER AS FOX

Today outside doesn't exist.
Today everything is in this room:
every time I shrank,
every bruised, broken, bloodied bone,
every Christmas card not sent,
every snide wrist limping into the shape of a joke.

I remember they said it was unnatural,
like queer was an inanimate object,
that the idea was incomprehensible:
a living myth, a creature from a book,
some wild, feral beast without a name.

She taps a thumb off each finger in turn.
Index, middle, ring and pinky.
Index, middle, ring and pinky.
I worry cuticles like splinters.

I was confused by how their stomachs sank,
how their skin crawled at something
that doesn't concern them,
but here we all were,
some of them feeling very concerned.

The scent of a magnolia I didn't see earlier
is sweet liquorice rose,
foliating into the cusp of a heart.
A cuttlefish disturbs the air,
iridescing as it floats by,
neon lights on zebra stripes.
Cthulhu if he went to Pride.

I chose to hold their prickled flesh for them
to ease the heft of my presence.
It could be seen as an admission,
that deep down I agreed
and put the bell around my own neck,
stitched the scarlet letter, wore the iron shroud.

A pair of bonobo dykes emerge from the fireplace,
buzzcut butch bois in well-tailored black fur suits.
A shoal of striped parrotfish
surface from my glass of water,
little polished ceramic totems,
boys one moment, girls the next.

Over time I forgot what I was holding
but never the weight of it.
It was pushed down further
by everything else life throws on top
until their shame sank deep enough
to eventually become my own.

A hyena stretches from beneath the coffee table,
pseudophallus dragging like a strap-on.
She curls up next to a lioness
whose mane shimmers like an off-the-clock drag king.
A throuple of greylags
squawk out from under my seat
while a fairy wrasse rises
like a tequila sunrise overhead,
transitioning by the time it reaches the far wall.
Flirting giraffe bulls stagger out
from behind the bookshelf,
necks wrapped in intimate embrace.

How do you expect people to change
when you're doing the work for them?
That shame is theirs to carry,
to reckon with those ugly parts of themselves;
why would you feel the need
to protect them from that?

I glance to see if outside has started to exist again
but can't see past the jungle now.
While it's full to bursting,
there's enough room for one more;
they're just waiting for me
to unzip the human from my body

and put down the weight
of that unskinned shame
and step out of it like a robe
to move into the wilderness, free,
queer as a fox in an uncaged menagerie.

THE WEIGHT OF BIRDS

Starlings flock to the honeyed roost
of an aspen crown in August,
bending its bows in depression curves;
leaves fix their grovelled heads toward the ground,
praying to a forgotten god of falling.
The curved bark, taut as rope
but with a little bounce,
struggles against the weight of birds.

There is a moment
when the murmuration ducks its collective head,
the wood creaks, lowers a bit,
and talons rise from their rest,
then all motion stops –
the grabbed lift of wing to air,
the tension released in an abandoned perch
suspended in expectant time.

Resuming, as if it were at war with the sky,
the tree corrects its posture
and hurtles branches like abrupt spears
towards the birds
warping and wefting like winged water.

My shoulders drop,
chest bright with splendour,
and I dare not
wipe my eyes.

LITTLE ACORNS

Every year, squirrels plant trees by accident.
Unable to remember where they've stashed their loot,
they build forests with forgetting
as little acorns left alone will bloom.

We hate forgetting, fear it even;
worry when we enter rooms without a why,
apologise for our tendency towards
tip-of-the-tongue thoughtlessness,
shamed when a 'good to meet you'
meets someone you've met already.
Twice.

I am struggling with this poem,
have squeezed as much of myself as I can into it,
but still nothing.
I fear I have forgotten how to do this,
so I put it in a drawer, walk away
and leave it be.

I wonder, when squirrels see those
seedling oaks shoot from the soil,
does an X reappear in their mental map?
Do they slap their tiny knees in sudden realisation?
I wonder if they know that by forgetting
they're flourishing,
fixing future food into the ground.

Days later, settling down to draft something different,
I open that same drawer and from its dark confines
out brushes a springy, thin sapling spine
with a handful of gentle, perfect leaves,
wobbly and lobate.

It's far from done and it'll need a lot of nurturing,
but it's something, it's here
and, bloody hell, it's growing.

PRELUDE TO EVERYTHING ELSE

The air here is delicate in endings,
with the bittersweet tinge of a blazing autumn sunset.

That was the kind of burning that heals, I say,
acknowledging that this is the last time we will meet,
a forest fire to cauterise my wounds on.
My visions of cremation were meant to show
that the wisdom of a scar
is that it's better than an open wound.

An ambulance shrieks down the street,
attending to an emergency you can point at.
I shudder a little; she replies,
I think you were so concerned with adapting,
you never stopped to consider that the soil might be unsafe.
That a body rooted in a suffocating landscape would rot,
but you've chipped through the strata of decay,
learned you were standing still.
You've figured out how to pace across the plains of your heart,
century by century, session by session,
towards the tropic of whichever sign you wanted to be born under.

Look, you've forged yourself against the embers' heat,
coaxed the fist of your pinecone heart to open,
and all those ulcerous, crystallised knots
that were swimming in your belly like razor blades
have fallen away
to reveal they'd been crowding a seed beneath.

Incense crumbles onto its wooden holder,
its plume rippling in the still air;
there is a sadness in today's joy.
It took bravery to immolate yourself like that;
you trusted through the smoke and smoulder,
having long ago decided that you were a funeral pyre
waiting to be lumbered into naught, but now
hold it in your core that you lived on past that sorrow.

I realise her notebook stays unopened
and that I have brought nothing but my body.
We are simply, today, witness.
Watch the years encircle themselves around it
and embrace the smudged, clean air with unfurled leaves.
Celebrate this as a prelude to everything else;
look at all the space you've cleared
now you've been charred from the crowded weight of yourself;
see the emptiness as primordial potential;
let the posture of the pines
remind you to carry yourself like you love yourself.

I step down the stairs,
through the hall to the door.
We stand, smile and say goodbye.
Her last few words follow my trail home.

Think of all the things trees see from their heights
and, being so deeply rooted,
how secure it must feel to sway
in the stomach of their own sunshine.

What progress, you ask, have I made? I have begun to be a friend to myself.

Seneca

PHOTOTROPIC

Clouds smoulder hearths overhead
with an almost-purple tucked inside their fluffed folds.
At least the shepherds will be happy.

I smile, awkwardly, knowingly, then begin.
I feel like I've developed a new sense,
though it's hard to put it into words
and I think that's half the point.
My skin itches for a sort of light,
moves itself out of darkness,
as if its reflexes have been remade
and crave soft glimmers
in the ashen barrel of spent triggers.
It's like a string unravelling from a bell in my gut,
hidden deep as a chakra that rings,
pulled by some invisible hand
towards the church of my intuition.

The charcoal eye of a Swedish birch blinks,
flicking a drop of haze from its eyelash,
flashing a tear against the silver bark.

I'm glad you feel it, I hear her say;
see an emerging smile,
eyes pinching at the corners,
and feel a bittersweet bloom.

She is not here, of course;
we are finished all that for now,
which has given me so much more to say
that must go unspoken.
This is just for me.

A squadron of Canadian geese
squawk chevrons towards the sea.
Spring is just around the corner.
I look up and inside I chime.

HAPAX LEGOMENON

a word or phrase that appears only once in a text

There is no silver bullet against climate change.
        Chandran Nair, correspondence, Nature, 2 November 2021

Tongues like triggers,
craving unobstruction,
turn inward, scouring genetic memory
at what ancestors would call this;
hold themselves there long enough
that sticky roots draw down
mulch-shaped names
and sort their emerging noises
as either instruction, sermon,
diagnosis, warning –
panning, really, for poems.

These hangmanned, haikued wisdoms
saw kinships hauled by companies, kings,
whose economics of empire
tired removing people from land,
so stole it out under our feet instead.
Reciprocity robbed,
repackaged into a resilience
required to survive harsh extraction;
those sickened, sooted skies,
exhumed mines, squeezed engines,
melted ice, acidic oceans, hollow forests,
crumbling dirt, shrinking coasts.

Can language seek beyond offset,
describe mending,
counter every storied breaking?
Could soil say anything other than spoil,
discuss, without addressing pain,
how bodies become powerful,
unshakeable sentences?

Bloody, boned hapaxes are we,
fleshed, furious skeleton keys;
actions alone, not words will set us free,
fighting shy one point five degrees.

SUPPOSE

after Kei Miller

Suppose we got this right?
Suppose we mitigated, managed,
manoeuvred and mediated
and arrived at cliff-edged tipping point
with enough space to take a step back?

Suppose we bought ourselves some time
to think properly and deeply,
to plan and imagine,
perhaps even play a little
and flourish the falling,
faltering from failure to failure
into fine footwork of a new future?

What if it all wasn't so hard after all?
What if it just took a shift in perspective
for its simplicity to become evident,
the diving board for all our choices to come?

What if working with natural process
instead of against it
made everything that little bit easier,
unlocking all the unspent potential elsewhere
in our liberated labour,
guided this time
by a more-than-human wisdom?

I would exhale
deeper than I've ever done
and sigh out the cobwebs garlanding my lungs,
catching the breath like a cough.

I would go outside and sing.
I would go outside and cry.
I would go outside
and the ticking in my mind
might stop.

FIT

Transforming in a matter of months
what normally takes millennia,
a wild design realises itself,
making me a different species of myself
by the time it is through.

It doesn't need me to fight to be top dog,
kill to be leader of the pack or
king of the pride.
It asks me to be
the plover inside the crocodile's jaw
who, unafraid of biting down,
learns that you cannot force your heart to heal;
instead you must allow it.

Survival of the fittest can be better described
as survival of the best fit;
as finding your corner in the wide, wild world
and learning the language of the landscape.
Life demands you pay attention to your environment,
supposes you are creative enough to make do
with what you find there.

These connections are our kin
in the family of the world;
we thrive in context.
Which is to suggest
that you will be the one
to heal yourself someday,
but that you will not heal yourself alone –
there is a whole planet out there looking for you,
waiting to help you find the best fit
within yourself.

ALDABRA ASYLUM

When the sea swallowed it,
I remade my home east
in Aldabra.
Catastrophe is a change
that displaces all refuge,
so I'll settle elsewhere, I'll retry,
but I'll always remember
and keep looking back
as I fly.

Never mind who I might become there;
imbued in my bloodline
are those guiding behaviours
of who I am, simply by design.

If the predators someday disappear
and the shores stay where they should,
I will land for the final time,
drop my wings
and flesh flightless into prime.

When there is no more reason to flee,
I will return from exile as if by magic,
home again, through all the bodies
born here before me.

AMANUENSIS

a person who takes dictation or copies text

It's not quite the same coming from these speakers, she thinks.
The bubbling chirp more Bluetooth glitch,
but this was the best hope
to pulse the honeyeater's whirring song
back into tradition.

Ever since that strident suburbia
sprawled them into diaspora,
displaced and depleted fledglings,
deaf to the ditties of their daddies,
couldn't catch the chorus
and, lacking conductors,
listened past the walls of silence closing in
and picked up instead
a friarbird's distant car alarm,
or the cuckooshrike's trilling slip,
but these bachelors' broadcast bombasts
fell on deaf, hollow ears,
for you can only sing
the wrong kinds of pick-up lines
when you're reading from someone else's sheet.

In playing amanuensis to these muted nests,
we've reminded those yellow breasts
how to incense their breath
with a protest against forgetting
and show ourselves
how love is the only mantra worth repeating,
because sometimes the solution
need only be as simple
as considering a return to form;
our muffled ecologies are just waiting
to spring into song

when we learn to let them.

HOW I'D LIVE THEN

after Mary Oliver

I would sit and watch those hundred rose-breasted grosbeaks
sweep charcoal patterns across parchment, weaving thread in a
rolling blanket of air, pinked with feathers and the tiny warmth
of a smile on the inhale.

I would ask the mockingbird for the wisdom he's learned by not
taking himself so seriously.

I would thank the bees for wildflowers and ask for their
permission to offer their liquor to anyone in need of a little buzz.

I would dream to that babbling brook and in the morning
whisper back all the secrets only sleep can keep and watch it
carry them downriver until they are completely out of sight.

I would write down those stars' names so I'd never forget what
they told me, would track their stories swinging across the sky
and calculate what all the fuss and hurry meant, to be prepared
by the time whatever it was they said was coming arrived.

I would step through the canvas of that painted tree and reach
my arms around its trunk, apologise for the dead flesh of its
illustration and remind it of springtime.

I would invest myself in the depths of that silver water, throw all
my greed into its deepest course. Would learn to speak about
value rather than cost, realise I am as rich as that rolling river.

I would ask if I could join those sunflowers and teach myself their
determination and spend the rest of my days growing towards
the light.

UBUNTU

Humanity is a quality we owe to each other.
Michael Onyebuchi Eze

In nature singularity is weakness;
monocultures are vulnerable to disease and predation.
We are no different, but we've allowed
invisible, unreal forces to plough our psyches
into neatly divided fields
of border, threshold and trespass,
forcing our attention to shrink down to size,
where the chambers of smartphone screens
echo each theory and every threat.

In nature, diversity is survival.
It gives ecosystems more ways to defend themselves,
complicates how predators and disease might break in
and bolsters the needy when it needs to.
It supposes that those brave or stupid enough
to strike out on their own
might bite the balancing hand that feeds.

We cannot crawl out of this mess
without each of us,
and we cannot have all of us
within systems that are unsafe for most.
We need each other to survive,
so forget *love thy neighbour* if you need to;
survival demands an intolerance to intolerance,
because it doesn't care about your bias,
belief, fears or nationality.
It is calling you to work together
despite the things that might keep you apart.
It's urging you to understand
the solidarity of symbiosis
is how we become fully human.

MAKE THE OUTDOORS GREAT AGAIN

Under the faint light of a waxing moon,
my mate Jess becomes a wolverine.
Keys nestled flat between her fingers,
teeth bared toward her palm.
She counts the tempo and changing distance
of a shadow lurching from the lamplight behind,
casting itself tall along her path.

Some days I am anxious to leave the house.

My colleague Mo turns into a fox on his morning run,
chased by hungry bloodhounds calling for cavalry
on tinny little smartphones, recording him like testimony
that he was existing where fur his colour shouldn't be.

Some days I'm sure the door is bolted shut.

Jude can't afford it anymore,
not when the electric's gone up
and the creche is bleeding her dry.
All she wants is a walk to gather her thoughts,
maybe sit and watch a while,
but time spent is money she doesn't have.

Some days its noise is a maze I can't find my way home from.

For Hayley, outside is a series of barriers
built from what others fail to see.
When she asks a friend what the view was like
she finds *beautiful* such a poor description.

Some days the ground beneath my feet disappears.

Chaz was a wildling once,
wished for nothing more than inside
as he slept between the cracks in the road.
He'd wonder what everyone's inside looked like
from time to time, bowing their heads
as they passed briskly by.

Some days I am angry at myself for staying.

Tom and Dave have been nomads once or twice,
unwelcome past the church gate,
the guarded pub door, the 'family-friendly' café,
outside made not with a door, it seems, but with a lock.

Some day it'll feel a little better, I'll be braver.

Alex doesn't feel safe out there, not yet.
Even though it's apparently all over
and we're getting back to normal.
He cocoons himself should he venture out
in masks and gloves and two metres of space,
but he can't control if others cover their face.

Some day, I think. Some day.

KAFKA DOWN THE HOBBYCRAFT

The emptied shelves would look apocalyptically ravaged
as I hauled every last one of their contents to the till,
the cashier curious but wary enough not to ask.
You get all kinds in here lately.

It would be like Photoshop in analogue,
stretching all my edges into PVA-perfected points,
a carapace of plaster of Paras
the right hue of petrol, acrylic blue;
pipe cleaners burst as antennae,
and a little bit of glue for extra eyes,
cosplaying whatever insect takes my fancy.

I would livestream prototypes and beta tests,
detail the articulation of a wing, its internal pulley,
how to make the thorax wiggle,
how to flesh the human into creature.

I'd check in with #EntomologyTwitter
for quality assurance and accuracy.
I'd test-run it down my street,
see how it fared in the open air,
watch the colours change under sunlight and streetlamps,
revel in the confused looks of startled children,
relish when they nicknamed me Kafka
down the HobbyCraft.

They'd see me there every day
like some sort of solo buggy Bacchanalia,
singing these insects' praises,
and I would march until the trilling,
buzzing, clacking and pattering
filled the postcodes with cacophonous percussions,
raising from the dead those composers
we never applauded enough.

BIOMIMESIS

Following a pair of well-prepared hares,
I step in from the glare of a Beltane sky,
feet softening on the blanket of a billion fallen pins
through the Scots pines' curtain.
Even in the spindly thinness of evergreens
there is good enough chemistry
bustling in the busy canopies
to taste cool oxygen on my tongue,
see my breath as I exhale.

I lie down, swaddled in a spongy bed,
and feel, not far from this secreted trespass,
the rumble of distant cars carrying children home from school,
trucks pounding from paddock to port.
Exhausts like blackened, open mouths
cough the dead into the air;
plumes of the past incinerate in an instant
that which died before this planet had a name.
What a pity, that everything that ever lived
would die to just end up as petrol.

There's enough fuel in these forests to last forever,
and it won't boil us in the process,
but we chose to build a future in a present
threatened by the burning of our literal past.

I didn't manage to see those hares again,
and there's a joy in how nature
will always be too quick for me to catch up.
Emerging from the shade, the striking heat
reminds me that a forest is a technology
when it's not treated as just a commodity.

TILL THE COWS COME HOME

Instead of milking their cattle year-round, [farmers] 'dry them off' during the winter, so they can calve all at once in April and be ready to go back to the grass in the spring. This dry-off allows farmers to do what had been unthinkable in the old system – take a vacation.

Janine M Benyus, *Biomimicry*, William Morrow, 1997

A landline rings through the empty farmhouse,
its tinnitus trill washing along the vinyl tablecloth,
catching in the net curtain,
calling like the ceramic mantlepiece cow,
whose mouth silently lows, wishes it could.

Outside, alfalfa has given way
to a succession of wild grasses,
each coming and going
as the soil welcomes and discards them,
reminding the tillage of how it used to last,
left now for Easter grazing,
cowbells pealing across the plains
past pats pulled into soil,
under sentinels circling seeds for snacks.

He got himself a passport
even though he wasn't going overseas.
The novelty warranted some ritual;
wasn't that what people did when they went away?
The furthest his father ever went was to the post office,
or a few times to the church down by the river.
He was almost disappointed
when no one was there to greet him;
that he didn't need to roll down his windows
and show his passport to some young
Glaswegian border guard
who's suspicious of English tourists in December.
All he got was *Fàilte gu Alba*,
and that would have to do.

He'd enjoy returning to his familiar loam,
but for now was free to come and go
between some new pastures of his own.
Free, you might say, until the cows came home.

NO OTHER PLANET WILL DO

If the limited series of this planet is cancelled,
I will demand one last extended special.
It might be a heavy watch with only a cult following,
but its characters deserve some closure.

Really, I want this planet to have its own cinematic universe,
for its phases to be neatly stitched together with enough spin-offs
that the transitions feel smooth and digestible,
for it to age with its demographic
without alienating new audiences,
to capitalise on nostalgia marketing with easter-egg references
and a million more sequels until we see how it plays out in full.

I want it as the only *Mastermind* topic of choice,
to be a *Bake Off* challenge every week.
It'd probably not win the lip sync,
but in a few years, when it comes back for *All Stars*,
it'll absolutely slay.

I would watch the livestreamed trial
of those responsible for centuries of its abuse,
our testimony exposing its roots
in the invention of racism, the ravages of empire,
through the insistence of patriarchy
into the exhaustion of capitalism.

I want us to be as excited about it as bitcoin, or AI,
but with less risk of apocalypse.
I want its name on my ballot,
invited to all the talk shows
and on the carpet of the Met Ball.
I want it to be the theme of the Met Ball.
It'll win Oscars in every category
and I want it on every unskippable YouTube advert.
I would whitelist this planet in a flash.

I want to unmute our WhatsApp threads.
I want it to Zoom call me without prior scheduling.
I want it next-day free delivery.

I don't care about the refund policy;
I won't be needing it.

I want trending stories of rich men throwing money at it.
I want a kind of migrant crisis in reverse
where the land welcomes home in tender arms
all its children displaced by climate change.

I want theme parks and studio tours.
I want every ecocritic cancelled,
an Instagram filter to show me what a healthy planet looks like.
I want to direct debit her every month.

I want these poems to be more than epitaph,
for each of them to be more than a vitrine,
but a postscript at the exit of the museum;
something hopeful, optimistic,
that talks about what's going on now,
assuring me it's still alive and relevant,
that there's somewhere out there I can touch.

I want this planet, only this planet.
No other planet will do.

HABEAS CORPUS

The inverse of all that pained hope
and brutal, soft labour
is respair:
the charity of rain after high summer heat,
the dawn's clarity after a deep dusk,
perhaps even the kiss of a breeze
wiping your brow.

There, the forest breathes testimony
through your larynx,
the mountain fixes firm your fearful feet,
and yours
is how the lake
becomes a body of water.

Again, you cease to be individual,
but this is the best kind of deselfing,
not a theft but the honourable giving
of a heart that knows where to bleed;
a return to the undivided you,
rehomed to where you were
before you were taken by living.

To be is to become,
to offer all of yourself
to everything more than you,
everything more than human;
to lend the land your borrowed body
until the dirt deems your duty done.

This nature, incorporated,
embodied, begins in wholeness
a path that is complete
when the forest speaks its *would*,
the river its discourse
and the soil has grounds for itself.

They ache in you
even now
as unspoken testimony
whose truth is filled when
its rippling voice makes all of this a court
asserting that what we say here matters,
what we are trying to keep here matters.

This is what we mean
when we ask for you;
we've been looking for you,
all of you
out there
with those beautiful, bold bodies
that hold in them the precipice
of everything changing.

REMEMBER THE FUTURE

*The problems of modernity are rooted in human alienation
from nature and are particularly expressed in hierarchical,
power-over social structures which disempower both
individuals and communities.*
Graham Harvey, *Listening People, Speaking Earth*, Hurst, 1997

What was scattered gathers. What was gathered blows away.
Heraclitus

Starlings murmurate overhead,
fanning their billowed circuit
above a river slithering out before me.
Rain pockmarks and dapples its flow,
falling like a grief shroud of mist
around the necks of these hills.
    I watch each drop cascade
    and spill towards the barren promise of concrete
    where dirt, too deep beneath the surface,
    sighs in thirst, watching water surf away in gutters,
    wondering: when will all the wet that came before
    trickle back down to feed once more?

It was once believed that after death,
as your soul sank to the depths thereafter,
you were made to drink from another river.
One sip and the trauma of dying would wither away
and you would be washed of its sadness.
They thought it a kindness to unsaddle that from us,
but in freeing ourselves from what went before
we fear now what comes after.
    A start we can't remember past
    and an end we can't see beyond
    turn our lives into eternal iterations,
    each rotation just a variation on a theme,
    ensuring that all the pain we've felt before
    will come back to sting once more.

Tempered and refined by the ages of progress,
the messy loops of our lives are hammered straight into a line.

Modernity moulded into monoculture
and restructured away from discussion, democracy and diversity
into hierarchy; a pyramid scheme society that tears us from each
     other,
forcing our identities to run parallel down timelines
to create isolated, partisan minds,
allowing competition to supersede collaboration,
and arms us with the cheat codes of consumerism
to fill our stocks with the time we've bought
like we weren't just living off the interest,
indifferent to how much of a waste it all is.
     What if our defining shapes could be replaced
     with something that leaned more towards survival?
     Halfway between a wheel and a line,
     what if time could become a spiral?

Look, here the regenerative circle meets the expansive line.
See where we'd observe what set the spiral spinning
and find where we excelled beyond the circle's bend.
     What's more, what if the course of these spirals
     didn't have an end?
     Not cut off as life leaves us;
     just let each bleed into the next.
     Would that give us a kind of joined-up, collective memory
     where we could think back beyond our bodies
     and become as wise as the last time we died?
     What if all our living lived before
     returned after death to teach us once more?

Would, then, each step be of progress relived and regained
instead of reducing what length remained?
Could it take this hastening along the plank
and curl it into an inertia of turning,
an adjusted orbit, a recalculation of trajectory,
an axial segue, a shift of degrees?
     Because although it feels like retrograde to me,
     which we tend to think of as moving backwards,
     a reversal, an undoing,
     everything is still actually moving forward.
     It just looks that way from this point of view.
     So how do we shift the paradigm, see things anew,

how do we learn the land as a living organism
and find our place within its ecosystems?
How do we balance our spinning plates on its widening gyre
instead of retiring under the increasing weight of our waste?

Is it too naive and simple a solution
for the planet to hold the very momentum of revolution?
It might sound somewhat idealist;
I have by no means a complete list of actions or plans,
just a notion, just a thought, just a vision
of moving on from here with a little bit more wisdom.
That we'll use the political power of personal decisions
to help us find a collective direction,
like those starlings flying formulas across the sky,
each following the closest seven.
Can we, like them,
amplify our actions to make a lasting difference?

In spite of our intelligence
we've strayed further from the elements than we might've planned
and, as the land beneath us grows shaky and unstable,
fearing what's to come as only something painful
is as useless as it is wasteful.

It admits defeat, surrenders to the enemy,
settles for dystopian tragedy
instead of tempting the spiral to open and unfurl,
teasing the past to come looser and looser
until we find we can remember the future
and that out from our amnesia
we'll uncover oracles in sepia,
where all the lives we have amassed
return to build something better
than just another modern past.

ACKNOWLEDGEMENTS

Thank you so much to the Burning Eye team for welcoming me back to your roster. It's a joy and a privilege to work with you again.

Thank you to Catherine of Nine Arrow for the beautiful illustration on the cover. I am so glad to have the chance to work with you. Please check out nine.arrow on Instagram or ninearrow.com to see more incredible Irish-language inspired imagery.

Thank you so much to my Wavertree witch Laura Brown for support and guidance on promoting and PR for the book. I look forward to the next time we get to chat and put the world to rights.

Thank you to Victoria McNulty for inviting me to join you on the road for two wild weeks. Our conversations and experiences will stay with me for a very long time, and I consider myself incredibly lucky to have friends in my life like you. Thanks also to Jess Orr for making everything about the journey an absolute breeze to arrange.

Thanks to facilitators and organisations for some incredibly valuable and insightful guidance: Anne Tannam and the Irish Writing Centre, Jen Calleja and New Writing South, Seán Hewitt and the Ginkgo Prize, Sarah Byrne and the Poetry School (as well as my fellow students of If Trees Could Flee for their steadying feedback).

Big love and thank you to Tina Sederholm, my poetry fairy godmother, for your kind support and affirming critique when I needed it most. You helped me unlock the trickiest parts of this collection while making me feel great about the work at the same time.

As always, to Rose Condo and Kieren King, my poetry parents, for the friendship and their own work that inspires me and so many others.

To Angus Taylor, thanks for moving to Liverpool just as lockdown was coming and keeping me sane. What a happy accident life can be at times, and I look forward to more adventures with you, my lockdown brother!

To Stephanie Lord and Abhainn Connolly, for the absolute great craic of our friendship, and for the sheer force of your writing.

To my Liverpool tribe, Emma Hulme, Amy Carrington-Spruce, Alice Mason, Lauren Buxton, Danielle McLauren, Alex Ferguson, Felix Mufti, Lyndsay Price, Ginni Manning, Stephie Gray, Amina Atiq.

To the friends I've had the joy of meeting on this poetry journey, Salena Godden, Joelle Taylor, Sam Grudgings, Louise Fazackerley, Malaika Kegode, Josie Alford, for your support no matter how long it's been and the joy of seeing your faces at a random gig.

Big love to Sheila McHugh for supporting our Outriders journey and making us feel so at home.

Thank you, Ben Mellor, for that wonderful experience of doing the Artists' Way together during the strangeness of that first lockdown.

Thank you to my counsellor for inspiring the character of the counsellor in this work and for all our work together that keeps this writing possible.

Thank you to my family for your continued support, love and excitement in my work.

Finally, as always, thank you to my partner Ben for your support, encouragement, humour and kindness.

CREDITS

'Remember the Future' was originally commissioned by Compass Presents for their Oracles in Sepia project. It has been reworked slightly here. You can watch the original version, with accompanying visuals, at bit.ly/3QWc0DE

'Euripus' was first published in *Blue House Journal #3*.

'Behaviour' was published in *Unpsychology Magazine #9.2*.

'Cianalas' was produced as part of the Outriders Project 2023, with Edinburgh Book Festival.

Various pieces were developed or started as part of my Writer on the Bloc residency with Writing on the Wall.